THE CHRIST-SHAPED CONSCIENCE

The Christ-Shaped Conscience

MYRON S. AUGSBURGER

VICTOR BOOKS

A DIVISION OF SCRIPTURE PRESS PUBLICATIONS INC.
USA CANADA ENGLAND

Scripture quotations are from the *Holy Bible, New International Version,* © 1973, 1978, 1984, International Bible Society. Used by permission of Zondervan Bible Publishers. Others are from *The New English Bible,* © 1961, 1970, The Delegates of the Oxford University Press and The Syndics of the Cambridge University Press.

Library of Congress Cataloging-in-Publicaton Data

Augsburger, Myron S.
    The Christ-shaped conscience / by Myron S. Augsburger.
        p.   cm.
    ISBN 0-89693-192-7
    1. Conscience—Religious aspects—Christianity. 2. Christian ethics—Mennonite authors. 3. Christian life—Mennonite authors.
    I. Title.
    BJ1278.C66A94 1990
    241'.1—dc20   90-37757
                                                                                   CIP

1   2   3   4   5   6   7   8   9   10   Printing/Year   94   93   92   91   90

CONTENTS

	Preface	7
1	Conscience and Christ	11
2	Conscience and Forgiveness	25
3	Conscience and Love	41
4	Conscience and Prayer	59
5	Conscience and Education	87
6	Conscience and Justice	104
7	Conscience and Peace	130
8	Conscience and Service	152
	Endnotes	175

To Esther
my greatest friend and my wife
with whom I have walked for forty years
in love and faith and growth in maturity

PREFACE

In the late 1940s I began my studies at the collegiate level of education. Although I had been an avid reader from a young boy, for example reading *Egermeier's Bible Story Book* through seven times during the year I was eight, and thereafter reading most every book I could lay my hands on, I entered college in many ways a very naive farm lad. The college campus was a totally new community for me. And even more so were the new dimensions of study. I will long remember one of my favorite theology professors teaching a course in Old Testament studies, standing before the class with Bible in hand declaring, "Your conscience is not the standard. Here is the standard; your conscience is to be standardized by the Word of God."

This is not a book on the function of conscience, but on the education of the conscience. To use a modern figure, the conscience is like the computer; it functions in the way it has been programmed. Our consciences have been programmed by family, church, peers, society, culture, and education. As Christians our consciences are to be programmed by the Christian community as we study and interpret the Scripture, applying biblical truth to the issues of contemporary life. We are responsible as thinking Christians to bring our consciences into harmony with the best understanding of the Word of God that our study and sharing in the Christian community can make possible.

Amazingly, with all of our talk about the authority of Scripture, it was shown by a Gallup poll a few years ago that the moral level of behavior among Christians professing to be "born again" was little different from that of the rest of society! What a tragedy. We are called to walk with God, to be disciples of Christ, to have our lives conformed to His example.

Morality is a matter of our behavior, while ethics is the science of morality, the discernment of right and wrong. Our lack of higher levels of moral behavior may be in part due to our lack of clarity on the nature and motivation of Christian ethics.

There are, of course, various reasons for this. Included among them is the fact that we have made salvation to be a simple existential assurance of being saved, rather than seeing salvation as a uniting with Christ in discipleship. Another factor is the general fear in evangelicalism of emphasizing obedience lest it be a "works-righteousness." We need orthodoxy but we also need an equally important orthopraxy.

A third factor is the inadequate place given in Protestantism to sanctification, to understanding holiness as meaning that one belongs totally, completely to God. A very basic problem in this regard is the manner in which the thinking and conscience of the average Christian is conditioned by the world or society in which we live. We are constantly shaped by TV, by magazines, by lifestyles around us that are of a totally different worldview than that of the disciple of Christ.

I grew up in a church which had a strong emphasis on separation, as was true of many churches four decades ago. While the concept of being separate from the world is biblical, we too readily move from an emphasis on being separated unto God, and thereby separate in and from the world as a controlling system, to the unbiblical position of separationism. What we need is a teaching and conditioning of the conscience that will enable us to be "in the world but not of the world."

It has been rather easy for evangelicals to say "Amen" to this concern when it involves the more personal, individual aspects of piety. We have been very articulate about things like truthfulness, not swearing, saying no to drinking, to dancing, to drugs, to fornication, to homosexuality, to abortion, and so on. But when we begin to address matters of conscience on evils that are more dominant in social systems, like materialism, militarism, injustice to the poor, violations of human rights, we find many evangelicals quite readily defending the conservative thought in the society around us.

Many discussions of "conservative" and/or "liberal" positions are far more culturally conditioned than theologically guided. Because of this, one finds at times that the secular mind is more open to, or respectful of, some of the higher Christian ideals in ethics of justice, peace, and love than are the minds of more parochial or fundamentalistic persons who have equated cultural and/or political conservatism with righteousness.

As evangelical Christians, we need to learn to "think Christianly," to think through the implications of various alternatives, to think with openness to the searching minds of other spiritually oriented Christians until we have brought our consciences into line with Christian truth! Conscience, I repeat, is like a computer—it speaks in the manner in which it has been programmed. Conscience speaks according to the way a person thinks. Recognizing this, Jesus could say, "As a man thinks in his heart, so is he." Conscience is the seat of moral judgment in a person's mind. It casts its vote on the side of what a person thinks to be right. But whether it actually is right or not is to be discerned by thinking with God in His Word. A thing is not right simply because we have "always thought in that way."

There is a great difference between the convictions of various persons, differences resulting from diverse cultures and patterns of thought. But one fact is universal: whether persons of different cultures think the same things to be right or wrong, the conscience still functions universally in the same manner; the conscience attests to the mind that the person is responsible for what he thinks or understands to be right. This "vote for the right" is what expresses our "free moral agency."

One of the serious problems in life is the tendency to deify conscience, to make it a god. Actually, we are responsible to educate the conscience by the Word and will of God. This means that at times the Word will talk back to our conscience, and will correct our convictions. Many persons have what has been called "an overly sensitive conscience." In counseling such, I have answered the person who says, "I suppose you will tell me that I just have to live with it!" with the comment, "No, I'm going to tell you to talk back to your conscience!" By this I mean to lay your conscience open before the Word and recognize that the Scripture is the authority. As my esteemed professor would say, "The conscience is to be standardized by the standard, the Word of God." We should, however, not play with the conscience, nor take its convictions lightly, but we should

9

test those convictions by the Word of God.

The Scriptures speak of the strong conscience or the informed conscience, and the weak conscience or the uninformed conscience (1 Corinthians 8 and Romans 14). As we walk with God, if we still have a condemning heart or conscience, we should recognize that "God is greater than our hearts, and He knows everything" (1 John 3:20). It is our responsibility to think with God, to have our minds and our consciences educated in His Word. This book is an attempt to help us educate our consciences.

Myron S. Augsburger
Washington, D.C.
1990

1. CONSCIENCE AND CHRIST

To this you were called, because Christ suffered for you, leaving you an example, that you should follow in His steps. He committed no sin, and no deceit was found in His mouth. When they hurled their insults at Him, He did not retaliate; when He suffered, He made no threats. Instead, He entrusted Himself to Him who judges justly (1 Peter 2:21-23).

Christianity is Christ." So said Oswald Chambers. What he meant is that salvation in and through Jesus Christ is the heart of the Gospel, and that walking with the risen Christ is the heart of the new life.

In 1964 I had the unusual privilege of conducting the only Protestant city-wide evangelistic crusade that, to my knowledge, has ever been held in Salt Lake City, Utah. We met for eight evenings on the capitol grounds, the front steps being used for the choir, and the several thousand chairs being set up before the building for the audience. As the evangelist, I was engaged in numerous conversations with leaders of the Mormon Church, even though they were not a part of the sponsoring groups.

After the first meeting, a spokesman for the Mormon Church went on TV to address the city. He said, "You may go to this

11

meeting—we need a revival of religion in America. But remember, we have all of this and more."

My task was to preach Christ with such clarity that it would become evident that they didn't have all of this, let alone more! It was for me to show that Jesus is not a prophet in a series of prophets from Mohammed to Joseph Smith! Jesus the Christ is the Incarnate God, not only a prophet telling us things about God. No religion can say of its leader or prophet, "You are like God," for no one has seen God and so it is impossible for any of us to compare a religious leader to God! As Christians we cannot say, "Jesus is like God," but we can say, "God is like Jesus!"

If you have met me and then you should meet one of my sons, you could look at him and say, "You are like your father." But if you knew only my name but had never seen me, then in meeting one of my sons you could not say, "You are like your father," for you wouldn't know. But you could say, "So this is what the Myron Augsburger family is like!" So it is with the Christian faith: we meet Jesus the Christ, and then we say, "So this is what God is like!"

Christ is set forth as God's highest expression of His person and His will. He is, as Peter states, an example that we "should follow in His steps" (1 Peter 2:21). That is, He is God's example for us. Jesus modeled in His life what it means to always do those things that please the Father (John 8:29).

The Christian conscience is not only brought to Christ for cleansing from guilt and to an experience of peace with God in the assurance of salvation, but the Christian conscience participates in a reorientation of its standards by identifying with Christ. The standard by which the Christian conscience speaks moves beyond the groundlines of the Ten Commandments to the truth known in Christ Himself.

INCARNATION

"The Word became flesh and lived for a while among us. We have seen His glory, the glory of the one and only Son, who came from the Father, full of grace and truth" (John 1:14). One of the most central and astounding aspects of the Christian faith is the declaration that God has actually come to us in human form. I repeat, we do not see Jesus the Christ as simply another prophet in a series of prophets, but as the very presence of God. Jesus said, "Anyone who has seen Me has seen the Father" (John 14:9).

As evangelicals, we often emphasize the deity of Christ but fail to equally emphasize His humanity. Because *incarnation* means that God actually entered the world in human form, we must hold two aspects of this happening together. First, for the Incarnation to be a genuine achievement, God had to actually become human, or He failed to achieve what He purposed—to be God with us. Second, for the Incarnation to be authentic, the human person had to actually be God, or else Jesus Christ was only a glorified man and not the incarnate God with us.

Theologians speak of "doing Christology from above," meaning to begin with the divine act of entering the world in Jesus of Nazareth; and also of "doing Christology from below," meaning to discover in the life of the man Jesus the characteristics which disclose the divine. Both are right, but separately they are inadequate. The two must be held in a relationship of tension, for the nature and meaning of the Incarnation calls for both aspects to be genuinely expressed.

The doctrine of the Virgin Birth has most often been used to argue that this Jesus so born must have been divine and sinless. Actually, it is more proper to think of the Virgin Birth as the declaration that the Word actually became flesh! That is, that the eternal Word actually came into the world in humanness.

Incarnation speaks of Jesus Christ our Lord, in one person the human and the divine. However, it is not proper to speak of the "preexistence of Jesus," for the human expression of the Logos had birth at Bethlehem in Jesus of Nazareth. But it is proper to speak of the "preexistence of the Christ," the eternal Logos as the divine nature eternally with the Father. John expresses this in the words, "In the beginning was the Logos, and the Logos was with God, and the Logos was God. He was with God in the

13

beginning. Through Him all things were made; without Him nothing was made that has been made" (John 1:1-3).

THE SELF-DISCLOSURE OF GOD

Revelation is God's self-disclosure. Throughout the Old Testament God revealed Himself in His deeds and words. In fact, the words and deeds of God are so inseparably related that we can say that God revealed Himself in His actions. Most of the self-disclosure in the Old Covenant brought us knowledge "about God," but in the New Covenant we meet God Himself in Christ. The writer of the Hebrew Epistle expresses this succinctly,

> God, at different times and in fragmentary ways revealed Himself to the fathers by the prophets, in little snatches here and there, and has in these last days [last in the sense of his unfolding revelation reaching its culmination] revealed Himself to us in His Son . . . the out-raying of His glory and the express image of His person" (Hebrews 1:1-2).

Throughout the Old Testament, God continued to disclose more about Himself until we come to Christ, who is the full and final Word, the full disclosure. As we meet Jesus we are now able to say, "This is what God is like!" The Apostle Paul writes, "In Christ all of the fulness of the Deity lives in bodily form" (Colossians 2:9). When we read the Bible, we do so to meet God. He reveals Himself through His acts in history, but above all through His presence in Christ. This is what we mean by revelation, an unveiling, a disclosure of Himself, and of His will.

God's full will is not found outside of Christ. This is not to depreciate the Law, but to see it in its place. The Law was "a shadow of the things that were to come" (Colossians 2:17). If you are relaxing in the sunshine and a shadow falls across you, the first thing you do is to look up and see who is there. The shadow is a sign of the Reality; we look for the Person Himself.

14

CONSCIENCE AND HUMANNESS

God became human without being sinful. This means that humanness and sinfulness are not synonymous. The Scriptures say that Christ was without sin, without the perversion of evil. This is to say that Jesus is the one truly human person that the world has ever seen. All others of us are sinful; we are perversions of the good.

Christ makes us aware of our sin and of our need of a work from God to make us new. Years ago Bishop Fulton Sheen wrote that we need to be born again. Just as a flat tire cannot fix itself, so we as sinful persons cannot free ourselves from our sins. Self-centeredness cannot be overcome by anything else than to become Other-centered, or God-centered.

Redemption, or regeneration, is in a very real way a restoration of the truly human. The Christian faith has the right to speak of humanness, in fact, of humanism in its full character. In Christian education we are enlightening the conscience to hold us accountable to be truly human by identifying with the example of the incarnate Christ. But we are fully aware that simply a study of the humanities does not enable us to live up to the best that we can conceive; rather, this study makes us aware of our need of divine grace to enjoy full humanness.

Paul based his appeal for unity in the church on the example of the humility of Christ seen in the Incarnation. In doing so he shows the interrelation of the divine and human in Jesus.

Your attitude should be the same as that of Christ Jesus: who, being in very nature God, did not consider equality with God something to be grasped, but made Himself nothing, taking the very nature of a servant, being made in human likeness. And being found in appearance as a man, He humbled Himself and became obedient unto death— even death on a cross!

Therefore God exalted Him to the highest place and gave Him the name that is above every name, that at the name of Jesus every knee should bow, in heaven and on earth and under the earth, and every tongue confess that Jesus Christ is Lord, to the glory of God the Father (Philippians 2:5-11).

This is the most outstanding Christological passage of Paul's letters. Here Christ is presented as the preexistent Logos, being of the same substance with the Father, and as incarnate in Jesus, being of the same substance with humanity. But Paul does not speak only to the ontological issue, the nature of Jesus the Christ; he speaks also to the theological considerations of the humility and the obedience of Christ in living and dying in the will of God.

CONSCIENCE AND THE HISTORY OF JESUS

Biblical theology has given considerable attention to the historicity of Christ, gathering the evidence, biblical and extrabiblical that He actually lived, and about what He was like as a person and what constituted His message. More attention could well be given to the history of Jesus, to the study of His person, His holiness, His character, His love, His deeds of grace, His ministries of mercy, His teachings, His relation with the Father, His patterns of peace and nonviolence, His proclamation of the Gospel and His unqualified faith in His future with God.

In his writings, Dr. John Howard Yoder presents a careful history of Jesus, showing the person and the expression of the will of God in the man Jesus.[1] In Christ we are confronted with the full meaning of personhood, with the full expression of the will of God, the example and unqualified practice of love, and the righteousness of life in an unbroken relationship with God.

While we may rationalize behavior that is beneath the level of particular moral laws, we cannot stand in the presence of Jesus of Nazareth without feeling the summons of conscience as we are made aware of our own sinfulness. Understanding sin as the perversion of life, we are brought to a more authentic sense of guilt when we measure our lives by that of the Master.

We cannot stand before the cross and witness the total self-giving love of the Savior and not be convicted of our own selfishness. No one of us can watch Jesus' nonviolent response to His executioners and hear His prayer of forgiveness without being convicted of our self-seeking. Nor can we come to the cross for personal forgiveness without being made aware that God calls and accepts us because of who He is, and not because of who or what we are. The death of Jesus, as well as His life, surrounds us with the conviction that life is far greater than our highly sought-after self-fulfillment.

CONSCIENCE AND THE RESURRECTION OF CHRIST

According to Paul, Jesus was a descendant of David, "who through the Spirit of holiness was declared with power to be the Son of God by His resurrection from the dead" (Romans 1:3-4). He was physically of the seed of David, one of us, a full participant in our humanness. But His resurrection certified His identity as the Son of God. In the New Testament the resurrection of Christ is central. He lives as our contemporary, extending His self-giving love in the presence of the Holy Spirit.

My purpose here is not to present arguments for the reality of the resurrection, but a few of them should be noted. First, the disciples evidenced a change from unbelief to belief that included pledging their lives to the death for Christ. Second, the first generation of Christians believed in the resurrection as fact. Third, the empty tomb is evidence for the resurrection of Christ, especially seen in the absence of tomb veneration which was very common in that culture. Fourth, the spread of the Christian Gospel and emergence of the church in various cultures is evidence of the living Christ. Fifth, the manner of the Christian pattern of worship centers in fellowship with the risen Christ. Sixth, we have the witness of the martyrs who testified to a vision of the risen Christ. Seventh, the experience of the disciples of Christ in each generation of history who "walk in the resurrection of Christ" is witness to His resurrection.

According to Paul, the new life in Christ is a death to the old life in which sin reigned and a resurrection into the new life in which the Spirit reigns (Romans 6). The sixteenth-century Anabaptists took this very literally and said that "baptism is for those who walk in the resurrection of Christ." Their emphasis on regeneration and the new creature that results from this led them to place more emphasis on sharing His resurrection than on the repeated confessions of sin in the mass or in the Protestant form of the sacrament. The resurrection of Christ certifies that Jesus is victor over sin and Satan, and that by sharing His life we share a power that counteracts the power of sin. This is not a claim to sinlessness but a claim to victory over slavery to sin.

As disciples of Christ, our consciences now hold us accountable to live not by a few religious laws but by fidelity to our risen Lord. Our consciences call us to fidelity, solidarity, obedience, and the joy of an open relationship. The conscience informed by the Resurrection calls us to devotion, to prayer, to worship, to stewardship, and to service. As in marriage, with its ethic of fidelity, so in relationship with the risen Christ we are held to fidelity to Jesus as Lord.

CONSCIENCE AND PERSONALISM

By using the word *personalism*, I mean to recognize the full value of personality. When we say "God is person," we are not speaking of God as a concept, as a mere power, or as univeral intelligence. While Plato may have reached as high as any philosopher in thinking of God as the ultimate beauty—the beauty being the rational, hence God being universal reason—this is not the God presented to us as the Father of our Lord Jesus Christ. The highest value is not idea but person.

The conscience, when educated in Christian truth, holds us accountable to integrity in relation to truth, to obedience in relation to doctrine or the laws of God. But it also holds us accountable to the higher level of moral awareness as seen in the value and meaning of personhood. We too often see the violation of persons under the religious claim of obedience to some particular truth. Not the least of these is in the area of male/female relationships in marriage; under an interpretation of headship, men have frequently violated the personhood of their wives in failing to see them as equally created in the image of God. Again, parents at times have dealt with their children in a possessiveness of ownership that has violated the children's rights and responsibilities as free persons.

This is also true socially. While rejecting violence in personal matters, many Christians have defended participation in warfare and the violation of persons' lives for the sake of some cause elevated above the values of personhood. While it may be true that in a fallen world, war is unavoidable, I find it hard to believe that Christians who profess to follow Christ regard participation in war as legitimate Christian behavior. In the sixteenth century the Anabaptists met at a little town in South Germany called Schleitheim, in the first Protestant synod convened, and drafted a brief doctrinal statement to unite the divergent groups into a common community. In article four of this statement they stated, "The sword is for those outside of the perfection of Christ." By this they meant that those who understood and followed the perfect will of Christ would reject the sword and violence.

CONSCIENCE AND KINGDOM REALITY

Jesus came announcing the kingdom as the rule of God. He invites us to be born into this kingdom by the Spirit and to come under the rule of God in our lives. He calls us to "seek first the kingdom of God and His righteousness" (Matthew 6:33). This rule becomes our highest calling, to practice the will of God in life.

Paul wrote that God "has rescued us from the dominion of darkness and brought us into the kingdom of the Son He loves" (Colossians 1:13). The earliest creed was simply "Jesus is Lord."

As E. Stanley Jones has pointed out, they did not say Jesus will be Lord, but Jesus IS Lord! Too many Christians think of the kingdom of God only in the eschatological sense of future events. They tie the kingdom to a future millenium so completely that they overlook the fact that Jesus as risen Lord is already exalted as King of kings and Lord of lords. Jesus said at His ascension, "All authority in heaven and on earth has been given to Me" (Matthew 28:18). As disciples of Christ we live now under the rule of Christ, we live now in the escaton, in the reality of that which is yet to fully come. Within a fallen world, we live as members of His redeemed community.

Kingdom theology is a worldview, a conviction that the risen Christ reigns in the lives of those who confess Him as Lord. This is actualized in us by the presence of the Holy Spirit, who is given by our Lord to those who open their lives to Him. In the sixteenth century the early Anabaptists taught that there are two baptisms, the outer baptism with water that doesn't in itself save or change a person, and the inner baptism with the Spirit that saves and transforms a person! John the Baptist said that Jesus would baptize with the Spirit. The One performing the inner baptizing is Jesus as Lord; the baptism is the Spirit we receive from Christ. It is His presence which actualizes the rule of God in our lives; He enables us to live as kingdom members.

In too many cases, Christians speak of "fallenness" as though it is our confession; it is our condition but not our confession! We are "signs of the kingdom," persons living by the will of God who become witnesses to the world that Christ is risen, is Lord, is in charge in our lives. Søren Kierkegaard wrote that purity of heart is to will the will of God.[2] Conscience is to be educated to hold us accountable to seek the will of God and to follow the implications of our conclusions in personal lifestyle.

CONSCIENCE AND THE IDENTITY OF THE CROSS

Wherever the will of God and the will of humanity intersect, we see the cross. Jesus lived under the shadow of the cross. He came to do the Father's will, and He knew that this would lead to a cross of conflict and suffering that would mean His death. In a real sense there is a twofold identity in the cross, with God and with humanity. For Jesus, the cross was a total identification with God in love and with humanity in love to the death. "The new covenant in His blood" was a covenant to the death.

In the atonement, God was doing something for humanity in Christ, and Jesus Christ as human was doing something toward God. The mystery is in Christ's unconditional identification with God in a love that would give Himself totally for others in His unconditional identification with mankind, a love that would suffer humanity's sin all the way to death. The Christian hears the Master's words, "If anyone would come after Me, he must deny himself and take up his cross daily and follow Me" (Luke 9:23). The cross we carry is not one of atonement, for that was completely accomplished by the one Mediator, of whom Paul writes, "God was reconciling the world to Himself in Christ" (2 Corinthians 5:19). For us the cross is a sharing of tension and suffering wherever the will of God and the will of humanity intersect. This is first within one's own life (Romans 6:6; 1 Peter 4:1-4); and secondly in relation to the world system.

CONSCIENCE AND SANCTIFICATION

The words *holiness* and *sanctification* are not prominent in much of Protestant theology. We have tended to speak of justification without a commensurate emphasis on sanctification. For many this has been because of a fear of perfectionism. Presbyterian pastor Bruce Larson has said, "Perfectionism will drive you up the wall," and again, "You can't be all right and be well!"

Holiness means that one belongs wholly, totally to God. This is also the meaning of *sanctification*, being set apart as God's own possession. When this begins internally, with the heart, the transformation becomes something that affects the total person. We say of the doctrine of original sin that to speak of total depravity does not mean that there is no good in us as sinners;

21

rather, it means that the total of our person is affected by sin. So, in the doctrine of sanctification, we do not mean that the person is now totally sinless, but that the total of the person now belongs to God.

Sanctification is given more attention in the Scriptures than it receives in most Christian churches. Perhaps this is due in part to the excesses of those who, in applying sanctification to a release from depravity, have felt led to emphasize a removal of depravity rather than to stress a release from the control of sin. It is better that sanctification be emphasized on the positive side of our belonging wholly to God, both the inner and outer person. As we belong to Christ, He in turn makes us to be holy. Paul wrote, "May God Himself, the God of peace, sanctify you through and through. May your whole spirit, soul, and body be preserved blameless at the coming of our Lord Jesus Christ" (1 Thessalonians 5:23).

There is a text in Romans that seems to rarely be grasped. Paul says, "For we know that our old self was crucified with Him so that the body of sin might be rendered powerless, that we should no longer be slaves to sin" (Romans 6:6). God deals with the old self by crucifixion; and He replaces the old self—that is, the life in which sin reigned—by a new self made in the image of Christ. Because Paul is a realist, he does not speak of the sin drive or sin potential as now gone, but rather as being devitalized. Our freedom from the old life in which sin reigned comes by experiencing the new life in which the Spirit reigns. The same power that raised Christ from the dead is at work in us to enable us to live a new life (Romans 8:11).

Our freedom is not in some isolated experience but in a relationship with Him; it is not in a one-time happening but in the practice of the Presence of Christ.

CONSCIENCE AND NEW COVENANT DISCIPLESHIP

Jesus established a New Covenant in His blood. As He sat at table with the disciples, He took bread and broke it, took the cup and gave thanks, and said that the bread was His body given for them and the cup His blood shed for them. While saying this, He was sitting before them in His body with His blood in His veins; therefore, He was saying in essence, "I pledge Myself to the death for you!" When we enter this covenant with Him, we pledge ourselves to the death for Christ and His kingdom.

Several years ago I began a practice in presenting the Lord's Table to the congregation that has become very meaningful for us. I took the loaf of bread and broke it to offer it to the congregation as a symbol of His body given for us. I then lifted the chalice of wine, but had a second chalice with water. Holding the chalice of the fruit of the vine before the congregation I recited the familiar words, "This cup is the new covenant in My blood which is shed for many." Then I interpreted the two chalices by referring to the fact that when Jesus died and the soldier pierced His side there came out blood and water, blood as the expression of His life and water as an expression of the depth of His suffering. Then going to John's first epistle (5:7), I quoted the words, "There are three that testify: the Spirit (God present), the water (the humanness of His suffering), and the blood (the divine life given for us)." Pouring the water into the wine, I said that as we are taken up into him, we lose our solo identity and find our identity in him! The beauty and simplicity of the symbol has continued to speak very forcefully to us in the congregation of the reality of life "in Christ."

Disciples are persons whose identity is in Christ, who live in covenant with Christ. We live as disciples, learning from, identifying with, and serving the Master. Ours is a spirituality of discipleship in devotion to Him, in openness to His Spirit, in learning from Him, in following His example, in serving others in His stead, in walking in the love and will He mediates to us.

CONSCIENCE AND SOLIDARITY WITH CHRIST

Paul's favorite expression of the believer's faith relationship with God is the little phrase "in Christ." This is our identity, our relation, our sphere of behavior, our meaning. As believers we have been bonded to Christ. In saying, "Jesus is Lord!" we are not simply expressing a doctrinal concept or an individualistic or internalized piety, but we are taking our place before Him as His subjects. We have joined the Union of the Kingdom!

While I am deeply committed to the value of denominational heritage as a laboratory of religious experience to discern authentic movements of the Spirit, I am convinced that we dare not elevate denominational values so high that they supercede our loyalty to Christ. In fact, we must be careful lest the symbols in such a heritage become identified with reality until we reduce Christ to identification with religious symbols that we can control! When we declare, "Jesus is Lord!" we mean that He is sovereign even over religion. He is Lord of history, Lord of Scripture, Lord of the Sabbath, Lord of the church, Lord of all! Even the word *Christian* has been so institutionalized and perverted that we should better be known as disciples of Christ.

Once the conscience has been "programmed" by the full Gospel, we cannot be at peace unless we live by the priorities of Christ. We are members of His kingdom, a movement that is not a structure so much as an identity, for there is no kingdom apart from the King. And when we confess Him as King of kings and Lord of lords, we are also declaring our fidelity to Him. We have no earthly loyalty that is at the same level as our loyalty to Christ. We take no oath of absolute allegiance to any authority other than Christ and His kingdom. This calls into question all secret orders, all clubs asking for absolute allegiance, all absolutized nationalism, all ideologies including religious identifications which supercede solidarity with Christ.

As disciples of Christ, we are not simply a people who are religious, not simply Protestants or Catholics or Evangelicals. We are persons who are bonded to Christ. Our solidarity with the Lord gives us our rightful claim to membership in the family of God.

2. CONSCIENCE AND FORGIVENESS

In 1973 I was in Bangkok, Thailand. Visiting the temple of the Reclining Buddha, I saw several Buddhist monks sitting on a bench reading a New Testament. I engaged them in conversation, and learned that a tourist had given the book to them. I asked them what they thought of Jesus, and whether they had discovered anything new that Jesus had to offer. Their immediate response was, "Yes, He brought the knowledge of forgiveness, and that has not been a part of our religion."

What would it be like to go through life without Jesus? This is the question thinking Christians raise as they contemplate the condition of their fellows in society. Being saved or lost is not a matter related only to the future; it is a matter of being in a right relation with God now.

Our society is so caught up in selfishness, individualism, and materialism that the larger questions of life are rarely asked. The issue is not whether we feel guilt, but how honest we are in recognizing it. The claim is made by some psychologists that many people burn up as much as eighty percent of their psychic energies keeping guilt feelings suppressed! One psychiatrist said, "I send my clients to church because forgiveness is taught there."

Some non-Christians say that if it weren't for the moralism

taught by the church, people wouldn't have so much guilt. But this overlooks one basic aspect of human nature—the conscience. For as long as people fail to live up to their own expectations, they will feel guilt. And guilt, like pain, is a valuable thing, for it is a safeguard.

In the Western world where we have had a monotheistic religion, we also have guilt, for we feel a sense of responsibility to a personal God. In Eastern nations where the religions are polytheistic, people do not experience guilt as much as shame. In fact these have been described as "shame cultures," for their people are held accountable more by social expectations than by personal ethical ideals.

In his book *Guilt and Grace*, Swiss psychiatrist Paul Tournier reminds us that we need to discern whether our feelings of guilt are valid or nonvalid, the latter being when they arise from wrong perceptions.[1] There are guilts that we impose on ourselves; some are valid and others are nonvalid. There are guilts that we feel because of the beliefs and expectations of others expressed in relation to us, and some are valid and others are nonvalid. And there are guilts that we believe God is imposing on us; some of these perceptions are valid and others are nonvalid. God is much more interested in forgiving and liberating us than in holding us under guilt.

"Father, forgive them, they don't know what they do," are some of the most amazing words of human history. Jesus was dying at the hands of wicked persons, and yet He prayed for their forgiveness.

The psalmist cried out, "With You there is forgiveness; therefore You are feared" (Psalm 130:4). This cry expresses an awareness that we are estranged from God with but one alternative— to receive God's forgiveness as the ground of fellowship with Him. This is the basis of our reverence, of our fear of the Lord. We are to be motivated more by love and freedom than by guilt and fear!

When we think profoundly about our relationship with God, we are inescapably confronted with our need of reconciliation. In fact, a personal relationship with Jesus Christ is central in the

Christian meaning of salvation. We have been estranged from God by our rebellion, and there is no way in which we can correct or compensate for that rebellion by our own efforts. There is no hope apart from God's gracious acceptance of us: the Gospel of grace is the good news that God is open and willing to forgive and to accept us in fellowship!

When we think of God as acting by the integrity of His person, we have to ask how God can act for the correction of human rebellion in a manner consistent with His justice. The good news of the Gospel answers that God's love reaches beyond the issue to the person, and that the change He negotiates is a change of relationship that deals with the basic problem. His justice is satisfied by His acting to correct the problem!

To redeem us and restore us into a right relation with Himself is a change God negotiates not by coercion but by the quality of His love. "For God so loved the world that He gave His one and only Son, that whoever believes in Him shall not perish but have eternal life" (John 3:16). God is defeating Satan and the power of evil not simply by the exercise of superior power but by the quality of His holiness. His justice is shown in the qualitative manner of His overcoming evil.

Reconciliation is the central aspect of redemption. Salvation is not a matter of our reaching groping hands in an effort to find God, but of our response to a God who reaches His hands to us. Salvation by grace means that God takes the initiative: He comes to us, He calls us, He forgives us, and we respond with faith as intentional action.[2]

At the heart of reconciliation is the experience of forgiveness. To forgive is the most difficult thing in the universe, and also one of the most unique aspects of Christian faith. Because other religions of the world, such as Buddhism and Hinduism, have not had a doctrine of forgiveness, they have needed to borrow this from Christianity. But their understanding is limited; to believe fully in forgiveness, it is necessary to believe in a personal God of love who cares deeply enough to forgive and to identify with us in the pain of forgiving and releasing us.

Forgiveness is difficult, costly, and painful. To forgive means that the innocent one carries his own wrath at the sin of the offending one and resolves his indignation through love! A refusal to forgive means that we keep the offending person as "beholden" to us, as obligated or indebted to us. To forgive means that we release the other person, that we accept the loss that has come to us from their offense, and let them go free. In forgiving we actually carry our own wrath at their sin and resolve this through love, refusing to make them feel our wrath and extending to them acceptance, love, and fellowship. God has done just this in Christ, reconciling us to Himself, absorbing our hostility into Himself, carrying His own wrath at our sin, and speaking back the word of acceptance. "God was reconciling the world to Himself in Christ, not counting men's sins against them" (2 Corinthians 5:19). This verse makes reconciliation central to the meaning and the message of grace.

THE UNIVERSALITY OF ESTRANGEMENT

The story of the Bible is that a loving God always moves into the human arena to call us back to Himself. God is at work creating a people for His name. In Christ He redeems and reconciles; He calls us into His kingdom and He owns us! We are now able to cry out, "Abba, Father," for we are children of God. We are granted the quality and the security of eternal life. We live now as His children and as disciples of Christ, as members of the kingdom of God. We are a new community, a community of the Spirit, a colony of heaven here on earth. This is God's answer to the human predicament of estrangement.

Our deepest sin is not simply the things we do; it is also in what we are, persons who have sought to be our own gods, who have rebelled against God in our quest to be totally independent from Him. Our fallenness is basically our separation from God, our exclusion of God from our lives.

We cannot expel the darkness from a room by fighting the darkness; we simply need to turn on the light! Similarly, we do not find release from sin by fighting sin; we simply need to turn to God! The answer to our fallenness is to be brought into fellowship with God.

As Christians, fallenness is our condition but not our confession. We do not surrender to fallenness; rather, we renounce sin and affirm our relationship with God by faith. The supreme expression of salvation is our participation in the kingdom of God. A social manifestation of this fact is our participation in the "redeemed community" as the expression of our identity in the body of Christ. Consequently, we find our direction not from our fallenness but from the community of the redeemed. This new community is described by Paul in his Epistle to the Ephesians: "For He is Himself our peace. Gentiles and Jews, He has made the two one, and His own body of flesh and blood has broken down the enmity which stood like a dividing wall between them . . . to create out of the two a single new humanity in Himself, thereby making peace. This was His purpose, to reconcile the two in a single body to God through the cross, on which He killed the enmity" (Ephesians 2:14-16, NEB). The redeemed community is the witness in the midst of fallenness that reconciliation is actualized toward God and one another.

SELFISHNESS AS REBELLION

Sin is the perversion of the good; it is the cheaper form of something better. Sin is not just things that we have done; rather, it is a perversion at the very core of our being that causes us to deify self and demand our own way. In this self-centeredness, we are persons formed in our own image, rather than what we were created to be—persons created in God's image.

The answer to our sin is not simply restitution for a few bad things that we have done. The answer is to turn to God and open ourselves to Him. All sin is ultimately against God. Yet we are sinners not so much for what we have done as for what we are: we are persons who like sin. That is, we like to have our own way. The most concise definition of sin is found in the words of the Prophet Isaiah: "Each of us has turned to his own way" (Isaiah 53:6). Sin is seeking our own way rather than seeking God's way.

Paul Tournier has said that if you diagram the personality of the unregenerate person, you should draw a large circle with a small circle in the center: then place the ego in the inner circle and a capital "I" at the circumference of the larger circle. To diagram the personality of the regenerate, you should draw the same two circles, but place Christ in the inner circle and place ego at the circumference of the larger circle.[3] The ego is still with the regenerate person but is no longer central; now, Christ is the center of life! We bring the capitol "I" back into the inner circle with Christ.

The ego-controlled life pushes the true self off center so that we cannot be what God intends. Christ releases us to be a more real self than we were ever able to be without Him. Paul wrote, "I have been crucified with Christ and I no longer live, but Christ lives in me. The life I live in the body I live by faith in the Son of God, who loved me and gave Himself for me" (Galatians 2:20). God's forgiveness is the one way in which we can be accepted by Him and in which we have life centered in Him.

THE DIFFICULTY OF FORGIVING

Refusal to forgive is a power play; it keeps others obligated, holds them under your thumb, and makes them squirm. To forgive is to release others, to refuse to keep records, to very deliberately decide not to try to balance accounts! To forgive is to affirm the worth of others, to recognize that they are far more important than the offense, and to transcend the issue in accepting and affirming them.

To forgive is not easy, because it means that we must rise above our feelings about the hurt we have sustained. There is something in us that cries out for revenge, that even calls such a quest by the name of justice. But the refusal to forgive is rarely a quest for justice as much as for retribution; for if the concern were genuinely a quest for justice, we would be engaged in correcting the problem. To forgive is to remove the emotional barriers that keep us from accepting the person and pursuing justice.

Forgiveness is liberation;
  valuing another, loving unconditionally,
  caring beyond the offense.
Forgiveness is substitution;
  one's very self bearing the other's offense,
  expressing in-depth love.

Forgiveness is an expression of our valuing another's dignity and worth even after a serious mistake. It is also our honest awareness that we ourselves make mistakes and need forgiveness. One who refuses to forgive breaks down the bridge over which he himself must pass! Jesus said that if we do not forgive others, we cannot share the forgiveness of God (Matthew 6:15). God's forgiveness is without respect of persons; therefore, His work in my life is to be extended in my word of forgiveness to others. If I refuse to forgive another, I am in fact opposing the work of God that He would express both in me and through me. I cannot have His forgiveness if I will not share it. I cannot enjoy His love if I will not extend it to others.

THE INNOCENT SUFFERING FOR THE OFFENDER

I was once told by an attorney that he could not accept the Christian faith because he didn't believe in the idea of the innocent suffering for the guilty. I responded by deliberately expressing sorrow that he would never have any close friends or a happy marriage. He reacted that he wasn't talking about marriage or friendships! But I pointed out that since he was not perfect, he would make mistakes, and only if his spouse or his friends would suffer for his mistakes and continue to love and accept him would he be able to enjoy meaningful relationships.

For the first time he saw that the principle of the innocent suffering for the guilty is central to human relationships as well as to our relationship with God.

> Forgiveness is at-one-ment,
>   the expression of mercy,
>   a gracious reaching to the offender,
>   divine grace atoning for our sin.
> Forgiveness is reconciliation,
>   a realism that acknowledges sin,
>   an acceptance that counters sin,
>   divine love forgiving our sin.
> Forgiveness is fellowship,
>   enjoying openness with another,
>   acceptance instead of perfection,
>   the oneness of unity in Christ.

The Christian experience is not simply conceptual, but relational. Only as God suffers by identifying with us in our mistakes is there any possibility of enjoying a relationship with Him. But this is the nature of love, the attitude that says in essence, "Your problem has now become my problem." This is not individualistic freedom. Rather, it is the freedom of the servant of God, the freedom to love and to enable another. The wonder of grace is that God enters into our problem, and "hangs in" all the way to the death of the cross. He doesn't cop out!

To forgive is the most costly thing in life, for it means that we carry our own wrath at the sin of another and do not make the other feel it! Forgiveness means that we are realists about the offense; we do not minimize it, but in our indignation over the evil, we resolve our anger at the other's sin by the power of love. This means that we process our wrath by a clear distinction between the offense and the person. In love we reach beyond the offense to the person; in grace we free the other.

The Book of Hosea gives us a profound picture of the forgiving God. The amazing story of Hosea and Gomer is an illustration of the cost of God's forgiveness. Hosea was told by God to marry a woman from the people of Israel, a people to whom he had been preaching with a strong word of God's judgment on their immoral lifestyle. After the marriage it became apparent that not only was his wife from a people of immorality, but that she herself was guilty of unfaithfulness. Gomer left the family and went to work in a house of ill-repute. When she was deeply in debt to the madam of the house, she was taken to the slave market to be sold. God then told Hosea to go and buy back his wife!

At the slave market, Hosea sat among the crowd as slaves were being sold. Suddenly his own wife was brought to the slave block, and as men began to bid for her, Hosea placed his bids, and finally, outbidding the others, he bought her. Walking through the crowd to the slave block he reached out and took her by the hand, and led her through the crowd and down the street to their home. In doing this, "he was numbered with her transgressions, the chastisement of her peace was upon him, and with his stripes she had her healing," words from Isaiah 53 which refer to Christ, but are illustrated by the suffering of Hosea to help us understand the suffering of Christ which was yet to come. This truth that the forgiving one suffers for the guilty is the meaning of the cross. It is expressed by Paul in the words, "God made Him who had no sin to be sin for us, so that in Him we might become the righteousness of God" (2 Corinthians 5:21). It is also expressed by Peter, "He Himself bore our sins in His body on the tree, so that we might die to sins and live for righteousness; by His wounds you have been healed" (1 Peter 2:24).

THE SCARS OF HIS LOVE

The cry of praise expressed by the myriads of angels in heaven is exaltation of the Son of God, "Worthy is the Lamb, who was slain, to receive power and wealth and wisdom and strength and honor and glory and praise!" (Revelation 5:12) In these words we have a vision of the Savior who suffered for our forgiveness, and who carried the evidence of His suffering into the heavens, appearing as the High Priest over the house of God (Hebrews 10:19-20). The hymn writer has said:

> Five bleeding wounds He bears, They strongly plead for me,
> They pour effectual prayers, For me they intercede.

The writer of Hebrews says of Christ that in the shedding of His blood, His death released His life "to appear for us in God's presence" (Hebrews 9:24). His scars are the evidence of our redemption, a witness that it is authentic, the guarantee that His suffering and death actualized the cost of forgiveness in history. In Jesus Christ, God actually suffered for our salvation (2 Corinthians 5:19).

Redemption was no mere academic transaction, but was actualized in history at a cost to the entire Godhead. The Father suffered in giving His Son; the Son suffered in giving His life; and the Holy Spirit suffers in giving Himself constantly to minister to us in our sinfulness. Pascal, the great mathematician and saint, once said, "Jesus Christ will be in agony until the end of the age, and we dare not be silent all of that time!" The amazing love of Christ is evidenced before the hosts of heaven and the legions of hell in that He bears the scars of His love forever!

In his classic work *Christus Victor*, Gustav Aulen presents the atonement as the victory of Christ over Satan.[4] Jesus our Lord entered the strong man's house to bind the strong man. Satan has been defeated by the quality of Christ's love and obedience to the Father. Even on the cross, where Satan poured out his final attack against Him, Jesus was victor! Satan crushed His body but could not crush His spirit. Even in the agony of death Jesus spoke the word of forgiveness as He expressed His love to others at the cross. He pointed a dying thief to the way of life. Even in shouting, "My God, My God, why have You forsaken Me?" as evidence for all that in letting Jesus die the Godhead was experiencing something utterly new. He yet in His dying moment expressed, "Father, into Your hands I commit My spirit!" Clearly Jesus was and is victor!

ACCEPTING FORGIVENESS

To accept forgiveness is an exercise of honesty and of humility. It is honesty in that we are confessing our sins and our need of forgiveness. It is humility in the recognition of our inability to restore or to set right what has been perverted. When sin is understood as the perversion of the good rather than thought of as "sins" being isolated incidents that we might try to correct, it becomes evident that this perversion is so total that we have no position of righteousness from which we can proceed to correct our estrangement or perversion.

Our human pride would like to make restitution for our faults. We would like to say, "There now, you have nothing on me, I'm clear!" But there is no way to make restitution for the basic sin of our rebellion against God other than to come back to God Himself. And it is at this very point that we hear the good news: God extends His forgiveness and acceptance, and welcomes us back into His family.

The story of the Prodigal Son is universal in its message. Each of us has gone away from God; if not in riotous living, we have done so in self-righteousness. When we "come to ourselves" and return, we will find a "waiting Father." When the prodigal returned, the father did not say, "Where have you been, Boy? What did you do with the money?" No. He simply said, "Son, it's so wonderful to have you at home!" And have you thought of what would have happened to the prodigal if he had met the elder brother with his unforgiving spirit before he met his father?

It is our pride that keeps us from forgiving others and prevents us from accepting forgiveness. We would deny our sin if we could; and even when admitting our sin, we prefer to make amends for it by our own deeds. But if sin is seen at its root as an attack on God, as rebellion, there is no way to make amends; we have to come to God Himself! This is what the Scripture means when it says, "Salvation is found in no one else, for there is no other name under heaven given to men by which we must be saved" (Acts 4:12). Salvation is not found in becoming rigor-

35

ously religious; it is found in humbly turning to God. The atonement is not simply a declaration by God, but is an actual reconciliation with Him.

WORKING THROUGH OUR SINS AT THE CROSS

It is at the cross that we understand our sin as an attack on God; it is there that we see God's love absorbing our hostility to the death and still speaking back a word of forgiveness. It is only at the cross that we can be fully honest about our sin, for there we see sin in its awful nature, in the full focus of rebellion against God. At the cross we discover what we really are as sinners, persons who reject God utterly. When we confess our sin and accept His forgiveness, our attitude toward sin will be forever changed. At the cross God joins us in working through our sins; one who works through his sin at the cross can never go back lightly to sin again.

Paul says, "The message of the cross is foolishness to those who are perishing, but to us who are being saved it is the power of God (1 Corinthians 1:18). When we come to the cross we experience release from our sin and shame, our guilt and burden of estrangement. Just at Christian in Bunyan's *Pilgrim's Progress*, when I came to the cross I too felt the burden roll off my back and experienced the gift of freedom. In my relationship with the suffering Savior, I find that Jesus is saving me today from being what I would be without Him. An old hymn expresses this truth:

> At the cross, at the cross where I first saw the light,
> And the burden of my heart rolled away—
> It was there by faith I received my sight,
> And now I am happy all the day.

In the Epistle of First John, the writer frequently distinguishes between sin as an attitude, a stance, a practice, and sins as deeds of wrong behavior. When we come to the cross in full confession, we bring to an end the old life of rebellion against God and no longer practice that sin (1 John 3:9), even though we commit sins of misdeeds, constant reminders of how our selfishness or sinfulness has so thoroughly permeated our lives.

The transforming grace of Christ releases us from sin as a power which dominates life. In our solidarity with Christ, we die to the old life in which sin reigned, and we are resurrected into a new life in which the Spirit reigns. This is beautifully and clearly expressed by Paul in his letter to the Romans, "Knowing this, that our old life is crucified by identification with Him, so that the sin potential may be devitalized, that from here on we should not serve sin" (my translation of Romans 6:6). Paul follows this by saying that when we are tempted, we are to reckon on the fact that we have died to sin. This is the power of intentional faith and intentional action, decisions that we can make moment by moment to believe and act in the will of Christ.

After we come to the cross to be saved, we do not then assume that we are through with the cross. Actually, when we come for salvation, we have only begun with the cross. From this point on we live as disciples of Christ who bear His cross; that is, we take up our identity with Him and carry in our persons the mark of this identity. This solidarity with Christ is a baptism into His death and a sharing of His life. The cross is the instrument by which the separation from the old life, the reign of sin, is actualized, and beyond which we share the power of the Resurrection.

In our materialistic age many persons seem to want a "sweet Jesus," a gospel of prosperity, and in no way want the "bitter Christ" who says, "Take up the cross and follow Me." We have moved to an existential or experience-oriented faith of "warm fuzzies" and a rejection of a discipleship that calls us to follow Jesus in daily life. But when we lose the sense of Christ's lordship, we fail to share the new life in His gracious accepting presence. We need to rediscover that the cross of forgiveness is also the cross that liberates. It releases us from our perversions to live in the fellowship of the Son.

37

Let us not forget that the cross of which we speak was His cross! Our Lord suffered and died there, in the ultimate expression of His identification with humanity. The Incarnation means that "the Word became flesh and lived among us" (John 1:14). But at the cross, He tasted death for every man (Hebrews 2:9). At the cross, humanity did something terrible to God and in the cross God did something fantastic for humanity.

"GO, AND SIN NO MORE"

In John 8 we read of the Pharisees bringing to Jesus a woman taken in the act of adultery. They sought to place Him in an inescapable tension between the Jewish community and the Romans, by asking Him to pass judgment on the woman, either by the Law of Moses or by the Roman law under which they were living. Jesus stooped down and wrote on the ground and then said, "If any of you is without sin, let him be the first to cast a stone at her." After looking around at the accusers He stooped down and finished His writing. What He wrote, no one knows, but since they were asking Him to function as a judge we can suggest that He borrowed the Roman pattern in which the judge would write his sentence and then have it read, so that there was no question as to what he had said. When Jesus stood, all of the accusers had left. As He asked the woman about them and she responded that no one was now accusing her, Jesus spoke to her of freedom with accountability. "Neither do I condemn you. . . . Go now, and leave your life of sin" (John 8:1-11). This is the word of grace that releases and changes us. We are set free, liberated for a new life.

When we know the power of the cross, we also know the power of God's love. Only at the cross can we experience its breadth (for God so loved the world), its length (that He gave His only Son), its depth (that whosoever believeth in Him), and its height (should not perish but have everlasting life)! This love that passes our comprehension (Ephesians 3:18-22) continues to transform our lives. The cross is our liberation, our new fellowship, our source of oneness in the body of Christ, for in dying to the old life of individualism and selfishness we are set free for the new life.

Peter says, "Since Christ suffered in His body, arm yourselves also with the same attitude, because he who has suffered in his body is done with sin. As a result, he does not live the rest of his earthly life for evil human desires, but rather for the will of God" (1 Peter 4:1-2). This means that the cross is the experience of transition from the old life to the new. Of this reality Paul writes:

> For what the law was powerless to do in that it was weakened by the sinful nature, God did by sending His own Son in the likeness of sinful man to be a sin offering. And so He condemned sin in sinful man, in order that the righteous requirements of the law might be fully met in us, who do not live according to the sinful nature but according to the Spirit (Romans 8:3-4).

The story is told of Abraham Lincoln going one day to a slave market to see for himself the injustice of the practice. A young woman was brought out on the slave block, her face registered her anger, her bruised body gave evidence of her having been mistreated, and as men made their examinations her eyes flashed with hostility. When men began to bid for ownership, Abraham Lincoln also bid until he bought her. Walking up to the slave block he reached up and took the rope that bound her wrists and led her to the edge of the crowd. Stopping, he untied the rope to give her freedom. As she rubbed her wrists for the circulation he said simply, "You are free to go."

The young woman looked at him with surprise, "What did you say, Master?"

Again he said, "You are free to go."

"Do you mean that I can go where I want to?"

"Yes," he said, "you are free to go."

"I can think like I want to?"

"Yes, you are free."

"I can say what I want to?"

"Yes," he said, "you are free now."

Her eyes filled with tears. "Then, Sir, I want to go with you!"

3. CONSCIENCE AND LOVE

In 1941 our family moved to Newport News, Virginia to spend the winter months in that area for my dad's health. He had a job as foreman on a construction project, building houses in a community called Ferguson Park, adjoining the shipyards. Bearing a German name and being a conscientious objector to participation in war, Dad was the brunt of considerable criticism. I well remember his accounts of Bob, one of his severest critics, and of the day Bob was laid off by another foreman. Some days later my dad created a few work places and went up to the gate where men were waiting, hoping to get work. Dad hired two men, including Bob, who really needed the work to care for his family. This deed of love was not unnoticed.

Fifteen years later when I was a young pastor, I was invited to Newport News for a series of evangelistic meetings. The first Sunday evening, when I gave an invitation to respond to Christ's call, an older man came down the aisle. When I stepped out to meet him, he asked, "Do you know Clarence Augsburger?"

I said, "Yes, he's my dad."

With tears in his eyes he said, "That man is why I'm here." That was the power of love impacting another's life.

The capacity to love and to accept love is one of the greatest aspects of our humanness. We were created by God in and for love, in and for community, in and for fellowship. We are whole beings, capable of entering into the intimacy of love. Love means that one's life is open to that of another. This means that we transcend the self-interests that may close another out, and we open ourselves to share in a spirit that includes another.

We are basically what we think. To "think love" is to think openness, to think compassion, to think caring, to think sharing. When we think of other persons as being important and beautiful human beings, as being like us made in the image of God, as persons with whom we can share and with whom by sharing we each become better persons, we are thinking love.

In this way we will find the key to intimacy, to opening our lives to others, to thinking relationally, to extending love to others, and to relating to them with integrity. Love will not violate or misuse another person.

Love delights in being in the presence of the one loved. When we are "in love," we would rather be with the lover than anywhere in the world. This is true also in relation to God. Love includes and complements and enriches. Love enables us to share with people in mutually beneficial ways for social enrichment, even if we are not especially fond of them.

The spirit of love can lead us to a oneness in fellowship that actually transcends personality preferences. Even when we are very different, we enjoy being together for the enrichment that comes from the corporate group. Such love draws us together in the community of faith.

LOVE IS PERSONALITY ENRICHMENT

"God is love!" is basically an action statement. God moves to us and shares Himself fully with us, no matter the cost. Love is self-giving, bringing to the other the essential qualities that complement and enrich. But we cannot turn the phrase around to say, "Love is God." The reality of God's personhood remains: it is God who is love.

While love involves the emotions, it is not so much something we feel as something we do. We love others and in doing so, we share with them. God's love for us moved Him to come to us, to share Himself with us, to participate in our problem of sin and to "hang in" with us even to the cross. When you genuinely love another, you do not "cop out" when the problems increase; you share with them no matter what the cost.

> Love is not an answer theology;
>   it is a relationship theology,
>   it is a theology of acceptance,
>   a theology of participation.
> Love is an invitation theology,
>   it is sharing oneself fully,
>   it is giving to enrich another,
>   acting in the other's best interest.

As human beings we are not like animals in the herd, which relate by instinct for sexual mating and for preservation. We are created in and for community, and community is not simple herd instinct; rather, community is a spirit of commonality in covenant. We are bound to God and to one another by the bonding of love. God opens Himself to us, and from this we learn to open our lives to Him and to each other.

In this openness we discover a bonding of mutual identity, of enjoying one another, of wanting to please one another, of seeking the pleasure that comes in seeking the well-being of others. We are human persons who can think creatively, love unselfishly, choose responsibly, and relate with integrity. We are given the privilege of belonging, of loving and being loved, of enriching one another's lives.

One of the most beautiful and succinct passages on love is the classic statement by the Apostle Paul in his letter to the Corinthians. Paul says that love never fails; of the triplet of faith, hope and love, Paul says that love is the greatest. In this most beautiful passage he lists positive and negative aspects of love:

Love is patient,
Love is kind,
Love rejoices in the truth,
Love always protects,
Love always trusts,
Love always hopes,
Love always perseveres,
Love never fails:
Love does not envy,
Love does not boast,
Love is not proud,
Love is not rude,
Love is not self-seeking,
Love is not easily angered,
Love keeps no record of wrongs,
Love does not delight in evil!

In Paul's letter to the Galatians, he gives us a nine-point description of the fruit of the Spirit, beginning with love. I believe it helps us to understand this multiple fruit of the Spirit if we see it as an expansion of love:

Joy is the feeling of love,
Peace is the practice of love,
Patience is the preservation of love,
Kindness is the expression of love,
Goodness is the action of love,
Faithfulness is the loyalty of love,
Gentleness is the attitude of love,
Self-control is the restraint of love.

"All of the law," Paul wrote to the Romans, "is fulfilled in this one word, love" (13:10). When we love God, we seek to do His will. When we love our neighbor as ourselves, we will not violate, manipulate, or misuse another, but will seek the best for each person. In love we will, as Immanuel Kant said, "treat each person as an end and not as a means to an end."

LOVE EXPRESSES THE IMAGO DEI

Love feels joy and delight in another. Love is an affirmation of worth of the significant other in one's experience. Love reaches out, includes, and complements. We learn love from God, and we are enabled to love by God. The capacity to love is a part of our having been made in the image of God.

> Made in God's image:
> What a stupendous thought,
> What a marvelous identity,
> What an exalted humanness!
> Made in a covenant of love;
> To share our lives with God,
> To share with another in the will of God,
> To be conformed to the image of His Son.

To be made in God's image is to have the power to think and to reason, the freedom and the ability to make moral choices, the potential of creativity and productivity, the emotive quality to share friendships and to covenant in love, the spirit to aspire and to plan, and the capacity to laugh and to enjoy life in praise or exuberance. Fallen though we are, defaced by the perversion of sin, the image is still there, recognizable in every person as the humanness that sets us apart from the rest of creation as God's unique masterpiece.

Sin is both rebellion against God and the perversion of our own selves, yet we are reminded by God and by our consciences of the good for which we are intended. In fact, the presence of a conscience, the judgment seat of the mind, is a constant reminder that we have an inner voice calling us to what we think to be right. The conscience, as we have emphasized, is like a computer, functioning as it has been programmed.

Since the conscience passes judgments on the basis of its conditioning, it needs to be educated in or conditioned by the Word of God. Yet even in the variances between consciences, there is one universal constant: conscience always casts its vote on the side of what one thinks to be the right. Therefore, to the thinking person, this vote is the indication that there must be a "right" and we need to seek to understand it.

Because the *imago dei* has been defaced by our sin but not obliterated, the *new birth* or regeneration is in some way the restoration of the truly human, of the true expression of the *imago dei*. We are being "conformed to the likeness of His Son" (Romans 8:29). We are being restored to the ability to be God's kind of persons who can love with integrity and joy, who can enjoy people without misusing them. Love enables us to be creative, constructive, compassionate, and companionable. Love is the dynamic of the new community God is creating.

The Christian community tends to look at eschatology in terms of the distant future; I suggest that we should look at it as the divine plan which already is shaping our lives. When we know God's ultimate purpose, we also know what God purposes to do in our lives day by day to move us in His plan. The element that keeps this from being a routine determinism is His love, His respect for our freedom to say yes or no to Him. This freedom includes the awesome possibility of a continued no to God with an eternity of separation from Him! His wrath is the frown of love accepting our freedom to say no, while at the same time evidencing divine displeasure at the rejection.

Rodin's famous sculpture *The Gates of Hell* pictures the cross. The only way in which persons made in the image of God, intended to share an eternity of fellowship with God, could ever go to hell is by tramping underfoot the cross of Christ. Equally impressive, as one views Rodin's model for this sculpture, is finding that *The Thinker* is seated at the top of the gate, chin in hand, pondering in deepest thought the destiny of humanity.

LOVE IS RELATIONSHIP

To love God with the whole of one's being includes loving God with the mind. This is an aspect of love that is too little understood. What does it mean to open our minds to God so totally that our very patterns of thought enable us to enjoy being children of God? It means to open the mind to God, to enjoy God's thoughts, to pursue reflections on life that include God-centeredness in our interpretation of life, to have a clearly thought-out worldview that takes God seriously as the first premise.

In God's created order, love has to do above all with relationship. Love is not a detached admission of a reality; it is personal identification with reality. In saying that love is the first commandment, Jesus makes clear that it is love that unites us with the Father, love that motivates us to obey God, and love that engages us in a mutual relationship of loving interchange with God. Love is active participation. When one cares enough to risk love, one finds that the risk is rewarded by a meaningful and transforming relationship. The fear of risk is actually an attempt to preserve one's life for one's self; in so doing, life is reduced from its potential.

Love moves us beyond our pride or self-centeredness; therefore, love has a redemptive quality about it. The redemption of the cross is the power of God unto our salvation, to move us from our selfish orientation to God-orientation. The new life which begins in our new relationship with God is a genuine inner transformation, a change from the dominance of pride, of self-seeking, to openness to God and other people.

Jesus said that it is by love that others know that we are His disciples (John 13:35). This is singularly important for those of us inclined to think that they will know by our way of articulating right doctrines. We may not know how to say everything we feel about God in the best way, but we know the honesty of our love for Him. We know and God knows whether we really want Him in our lives; whether, as Canon Bryan Green has said, "Our face is toward God or our back is toward God."

LOVE IS SELFLESS INTIMACY

Love is covenant power, the ability to enter a relationship with another on a basis of equality of worth and of shared responsibility, with mutual obligation to give and receive without using the other. In this covenant we recognize one another's true worth. In this relationship we affirm the importance of the other, and in this covenant we give unqualified love.

Love is seen in its higher social expression in the covenant relationship of marriage. In Ephesians 5, Paul makes clear that such a covenant involves mutual submission, mutual love, and mutual respect. This passage does not teach "chain of command," a term which is more military than biblical. The wife is to submit to her husband as unto the Lord Christ; that is, in an attitude of enhancing his role as she confesses her unqualified commitment. In turn, the husband is to give himself to and for his wife as totally as Christ has given Himself to the death for the church. Such mutual submission enables the enrichment of mutual love; and in such love, there follows the mutual respect in which marriage is "the queen of friendships."

In his first letter to the Corinthians, Paul teaches that man and woman are to relate as God and Christ relate (11:3). To say that Christ is inferior to God would be heresy; just so, to say that woman is inferior to man is a heresy.[1]

In marriage, love is not static but a dynamic, enriching partnership. In the ideal marriage we covenant together in trusting, grow together in loving, and mature together in sharing. Marriage is not a limitation but an expansion of life; it is not competition but a friendship. The couple sharing a maturing relationship will avoid the polarization of driving one another to opposite extremes, and will support one another rather than embarrass or depersonalize the other.

Our love in marriage is more than sexual harmony; it is a whole life reflection of the total self-giving love of Christ for us. This intimacy will serve to enrich the lives of others as we share in the covenant community. "No man is an island" may refer to the way in which we contribute to others as well as to how we receive and are enriched by our association with others.

> Intimacy is openness to another;
> sharing the whole personality,

enjoying the interchange of thought,
   the peace of emotional belonging,
   the togetherness of being one.
Intimacy is holistic respect;
   relating in implicit trust,
   sharing in harmony of purpose,
   being open and pure in motive,
   accepting another's strength.

In the redeemed community, we extend love not as sexual experience but as the intimacy that is the enjoyment of one another in the spirit of Christ. This intimacy means taking seriously the importance and value of persons. I have often been convicted by the words of the late Dr. Samuel Shoemaker, Episcopal rector of New York and Pittsburgh: "There is enough time in every day to treat each person as a person."

Our lack of intimacy is in part due to our not taking time to share with others, to include them in our circle of people important to us, to open ourselves to them in the depth of covenant love in which we fully trust each other. The reward of intimacy is the deep sense of belonging, of being understood and cared for, of being able to share completely without the fear of rejection.

Jesus expressed this intimacy in his friendship with Martha, Mary, and Lazarus, enjoying time with them. My wife, Esther, recently did an abstract sculpture of Mary wiping Jesus' feet with her hair. The lines and movement in the sculpture take the viewer beyond the artistic creativity and beauty to the devotion expressed by Mary's act. This love between Jesus and this family was a bond in which each delighted. It is the nature of love that it enjoys being with the person loved, bringing them pleasure, seeking their good and fulfillment.

Love is concern for others,
   action that evidences caring,
   action designed for peace,
   action designed in justice.

Love is seen fully in the Incarnation,
  for the Word became flesh among us,
  God's action in self-giving love,
  God's giant step across the barrier!

Love takes the initiative in building relationships. It finds the way into another's life, constructing bridges that cross barriers. But love does this in a spirit that engages another without manipulating or coercing. Love respects others, participating in their sphere without insisting that they respond to our agenda. Jesus, the incarnate Son of God, moved among people expressing His love and caring for people while at the same time respecting their freedom to reject or accept Him.

Love is enjoying persons, wanting to be with them, wanting to share. It is recognizing their worth and affirming it. The attitude shapes the act. When love is genuine, it brings the two together, attitude and act, in one expression of self-giving. We learn from God what it means to love without conditions, to love for the good of others and not for self-interest. Love moves us to participate in the lives of others as they voluntarily open themselves to us. Love seeks their fulfillment even at a cost to ourselves. Love doesn't need to win! We share, not to conquer but to participate.

Love of another includes joy in his or her successes as well as participation in problems. To love is to share with them, even in their difficulties; however, this does not mean carrying their problems and thereby increasing their dependency. To share love with another is to work with them, to counsel, to support, to help find the way to resolve an issue; but it does not take their responsibility to act as a responsible person. "Agape" love liberates a person to be a true self with a high sense of worth.

Love is more than selfish passion,
  than possessing another,
  than frolicking together,
  than emotional bonding.
Although love is all of this, it is more.

Love is more deeply seen in suffering,
    where trials unite,
    where pain engages,
    where difficulties mature us,
for love is this—and more.

Love is a spiritual bonding,
    becoming one in spirit,
    processing difficulties together,
    rejoicing in common goals,
for love is sharing each other with God!

Someone has said that we should embrace our friends and embrace our enemies even more closely! The embrace of love can make friends of those enemies. As God in love moved to us when we were enemies, so we in love move to others to overcome enmity. We do not accept enmity as final in any human sphere. The cross is central in the Christian faith, and yet we often fail to see the cost of the love that was expressed in the cross, in Christ dying for His enemies. From the human perspective, love did not win, for He died. But from a post-resurrection perspective, we see that Christ's love absorbed all of the hostility of His enemies with an integrity that didn't strike back, but demonstrated the power to keep on caring, no matter what the cost. He was and is victor of spirit.

When we take Jesus seriously we cannot but take seriously His spirit and model of love. If we are Christocentric in our interpretation of the Scripture, we will invariably see the relevance of nonviolence, or of nonresistance in human relationships. In nonviolence we keep interpersonal relations on a level that permits the richness of the interchange of personalities, the dialogue and understandings that can enrich rather than destroy. Violence leads to death, and death is so final . . . we lose the person who is destroyed, we are forever the poorer for the loss of a potential friend.

God has chosen to bind Himself to the practice of love, working patiently to see that His victory is one of quality rather than dominance, and one of transformation rather than of subjugation. For the 2,000 years since the cross of Christ, God has continued to relate to humanity on the ground of the cross. Calvary is the one place where we can be honest about the full nature of our sin against God, and where we observe the full nature of Christ's love. God's love redeems by liberating, by freeing us to become children of God!

Love cost God the cross. To identify with us in our sinfulness, there was no authentic way of sharing our problem without sharing the meaning of sin's extrangement and resultant death. When we truly care for others, truly love, a little of Calvary is expressed again. We die to ourselves and open ourselves to others in the throbbing, participating, often suffering love that is known in the cross. As we become involved in costly caring, the love and pain of the cross become real in our own lives.

LOVE IS SOMETHING WE FEEL

Sweet aroma filled the room as Mary knelt at the foot of the cot on which Jesus reclined to eat, pouring her gift of expensive perfume over His feet and wiping them with her hair. This was her expression of love, her act of total devotion. She knew this Christ: she had been forgiven and released by Him, she had been included in His circle of friends, accepted by Him as a person of worth! Her behavior was radically different from what it might earlier have been when she was a "public woman." This was an act of repentant, loving, serving devotion.

From this act of devotion Jesus drew for Simon, His host, the life-transforming lesson that speaks to each of us. Love is something we feel, but it is not irrational; it is simply its own language of relationship and of affirmation which goes beyond words. Thinking people love, and if they do not, they have failed to think adequately, for thinking is to include the whole of personality. We are made with the capacity to love, to covenant, to participate with the spirit and mind and body and soul. We do not separate the mind from the rest of the personality. In fact, it takes soundness of mind to be able to truly love; mental disharmony incapacitates one's ability to love genuinely. Love involves holistic caring, a participation with others that is unselfish and in no way exploitive.

> Love is expressed by the compassionate life:
>   a life that points beyond itself,
>   a life experienced in a community of faith,
>   a life that partakes of the New Order. . . .
> Love as compassion calls us to suffer:
>   to identify with those who hurt,
>   to cry with those in misery,
>   to be vulnerable with the vulnerable.

Love carries the risk of giving oneself totally and being ignored or rejected; the risk of entering covenant only to find that the other was incapable of authentic covenanting. Some persons would much rather have a contract to guarantee "fairness" to their own interests, a way out if the relationship should become too demanding and costly. But authentic love carries with it the risks of partnership and trust, of suffering and thereby maturing together.

Love does not seek dominion but development; it does not seek control but companionship; it does not seek to manipulate but to mature; it does not seek headship but provides it in service that fulfills both together. Dominion theology, which has become popular in some circles of the Christian church, stands in contrast to a theology of love and service. God does not call us to have dominion over other people, but to serve.

The commandment in Genesis was for humanity to have dominion over the created order of the world that we call nature, and to be responsible and good stewards over resources of the environment. But the first family was not to have dominion over other peoples. Cain tried to dominate Abel and it didn't work; he tried to be his brother's keeper when he should have been his brother's brother! Love relates, liberates, enables, and enriches, but love does not dominate.

The ability to feel love is threatened by competitive patterns, selfishness, and materialism. In the pursuit of financial power and material security, we enjoy playing god over the things which we own; and the more we play god, the more we come to think we are gods. From such a self-made throne, we find it impossible to step down and to "wash another's feet," or make ourselves vulnerable.

We are accustomed to controlling what we own, and we extend this control into our relations with others. The subtle thing about materialism is in the spirit of controlling, of being "in charge." This is what makes it hard for a rich man to become engaged in the kingdom of God! But, as Jesus said, "All things are possible with God" (Mark 10:27).

The Christian faith presents a unique ethic of love. The human mind tends to legalism, perhaps not so much because of the nature of the function of our intellects, but because of the nature of our sinfulness in that we instinctively want to control issues, things, and persons. In love we do not control, we relate. In love we do not violate. We will not rob others of life by killing. We will not violate covenant in committing adultery. We will not steal. We will not bear false witness. We will not covet. In understanding love in the dimensions of this second table of the Law, we have clear and effective correctives to child abuse, to violence, to immorality, to taking anything that rightfully belongs to another. Love is solidarity with others. As God shares in solidarity with us, in our problems, in our questions, in our confusion; so we share in solidarity with others, in common weakness, in shared powerlessness, in mutual vulnerability.

The love ethic is not simply an ethical principle tacked on to our materialistic philosophy of life in the hope of sanctifying our pattern; rather, it is the dynamic worldview of the disciple of Christ. Love is a way of life, the central aspect of Christian character, the power that relates us authentically to God and genuinely to our sisters and brothers.

The larger issue of Christian faith is answered when we respond to the questions, "How do I feel about God? Do I want God in my life? Am I willing to let God be God in my life?" We may have many unanswered questions about God, but we need not wait for all of the answers to decide that we want to know God and to have Him in our lives. The German poet Goethe once said, "Give me the benefit of your convictions, if you have any, but keep your doubts to yourself, for I have enough of my own."

It is the conviction that God loves us, and has taken the initiative, and comes to us, that brings meaning into our lives. It was this awareness that led the twelfth-century theologian Anselm to affirm, "Faith seeks understanding." Assurance of salvation and security in Christ is above all the awareness that we are accepted by God and adopted into His family.

LOVE IS A CORRECTIVE FOR VIOLENCE

Do not repay anyone evil for evil. Be careful to do what is right in the eyes of everybody. If it is possible, as far as it depends on you, live at peace with everyone. Do not take revenge, my friends, but leave room for God's wrath, for it is written: "It is mine to avenge; I will repay," says the Lord. On the contrary: If your enemy is hungry, feed him; if he is thirsty, give him something to drink. In doing this, you will heap burning coals on his head. Do not be overcome by evil, but overcome evil with good (Romans 12:17-21).

This passage is very similar in content to the ethical teachings of Jesus. His Sermon on the Mount is kingdom preaching that calls us into a new freedom to live as disciples of Christ. Jesus, as victor, has liberated us from our bonds and invites us to walk with Him in a new freedom. This freedom calls us to hear the Sermon on the Mount as nothing but Gospel. As Eduard Thurneysen has said, "Here 'living' and 'believing,' 'believing' and 'living,' are of equal weight and thus merge into one."[2]

As a post-resurrection convert to Christ, the Apostle Paul helps us to see the relation of the Sermon to the Sermonizer. We do not detach themes of the Sermon from the Christ, but we hold its teachings as the Gospel of Christ, to be lived only in and by relationship with Christ.

The Sermon on the Mount was given us by the Christ, the Messiah, expressing the way in which the disciple or kingdom member will conduct life. In the Roman passage, Paul is similarly expressing how the person who is "in Christ," who has identity in Him, who is actually reconciled to God in Christ, will conduct his or her life! These are the standards by which we are to educate our conscience.

There are two distinctions which I must make here. The first is between the "already" and the "not yet" of the kingdom of heaven. While the "rule of God" is happening in the life of the disciple, it is "not yet" fully here but it is yet coming; and because it is coming both immediately and futuristically, it is to be announced. The life of discipleship is such an annunciation, for the conviction of the "not yet" of the kingdom to come "already" shapes the lives of those of us who take Christ and His kingdom seriously. We are heralds of the kingdom, living by the kingdom principles now.

The second distinction that must be made is between the disciples and the world, a separation unto God for those who identify with Christ and share a resultant separation in the world. This means that the Christian ethic of love and nonviolence is an ethic for the community of the King, expected of the disciples of Christ; but it is not an ethic that can be forced upon or expected from those who are not Christ's disciples. The nondisciple lives at another level of life, not answering to the authority of Christ but to the will of men. One becomes a kingdom member by a voluntary response to Christ's call.

The ethic of love, as Jesus presented it, is more positive than negative. Jesus' commandments are a key to becoming what we are as members of the kingdom of Christ. We are to read the Sermon on the Mount, and the ethical passages of the New Testament in the way in which Karl Barth interprets Matthew 6:24, not as "You shall not," but as "You cannot"; that is, "You cannot serve God and mammon." There is no way in which you can do this — it doesn't work! In the ethics of the Gospel, you cannot hate your enemies, you cannot betray your covenant by adultery, and you cannot live unjustly. The new holiness consists of being completely devoted to Christ and His will.

Evangelical Christians often read the word *pacifism* as being an impossible and irrelevant idealism rather than a strategy of life for the disciple of Christ. But pacifism lived in Christian love is anything but passive; for love is an action of matching a violent spirit with a loving spirit. It is an attitude and action that engages the opponent by demonstrating a life-changing ethic, even though we suffer in doing so. I need scarcely remind us that the use of violence does not in any way assure us that we will not suffer. The issue, however, is not to avoid suffering but to avoid the compromise of life-values.

LOVE IS COMPASSIONATE PARTICIPATION

Share with God's people who are in need. Practice hospitality. Bless those who persecute you; bless and do not curse. Rejoice with those who rejoice; mourn with those who mourn. Live in harmony with one another. Do not be proud, but be willing to associate with people of low position. Do not be conceited (Romans 12:13-16).

To love is to act in the spirit of Jesus. There is a Christian order of life for each of us who take with utmost seriousness the call to follow Jesus. Having been laid hold of by God in grace, we bear testimony to the righteousness of Christ into which we have been called and in which we are continuously being transformed. In all aspects of the will of God, even in the more minute of His commandments, we must seek only Jesus and His Spirit, or our righteousness will be no better than that of the scribes and Pharisees (Matthew 5:19-20).

Only as the branch abides in the Vine can it bear fruit, and we are branches of the one Vine, Jesus Christ (John 15:1-8). As we abide in Him, the same life-flow of God will be expressed in us that was expressed in His life, for we are to walk as Jesus walked (1 John 2:6). In my opinion this is not a "token obedience," a symbolic deed, but a genuine obedience of faith in which we obey as best we can by the power of His Spirit, while at the same time exercising faith that He accepts our obedience, imperfect as it is, because of our identification with Christ.

Love is not primarily a morality, but a mode of being. Our tendency in the church is to set up a system of morality and in doing so to reject the Gospel. When we elevate a code of morality above faith, hope, and love, we eclipse the Gospel. One of the more serious problems for the church is the substitution of "good views" for "Good News." The correction of ethical or moral disorder is not found in becoming more moralistic; it is found in forgiving and transforming grace that enables a disciple to live "after the power of an endless life."

A lack of grace results in Christians failing to have compassion, first toward themselves and then toward others. Only in an experience of God's unqualified love and accepting grace can we accept others in compassion. Grace exposes without rejecting; in a sense, it judges without being judgmental; it faces sin realistically and still moves beyond the sin to the sinner in forgiving, accepting love.

Compassion does not mean that we can or should do everything for the other, but it means that we have an attitude of acceptance and in-depth caring. Love is personal power shared with others for their enrichment. Love is justice spread around for the well-being of others. Love is hope in action, the expression that we believe that things need not stay as they are, that they can be changed. Love is peace impacting others in spirit, for love demonstrates that one's spirit can be victorious in the most trying situation. Love is an essential element of the Gospel.

We must think love if we are to fully participate in love. As we share love with others, we think loving expressions and smile love's acceptance. Love is a universal language. Love is God's communication of Himself. Love is our communication of a genuine participation with God.

4. CONSCIENCE AND PRAYER

As a young lad growing up on a farm in western Ohio, I was one of a family of six children, five boys and one girl. We lived on a small farm, and did mostly truck-farming, growing about eight acres of melons each summer as one of our cash crops. When I was about six years of age and young enough that I was not yet asked to handle the hoe, it was my lot to carry drinking water to my dad and two older brothers.

One hot day, arriving among them in the melon field, I heard them complaining about how dry it was and how much they needed rain. I very presumptuously said, "Well, why don't you pray for rain?" My older brother turned to me with the comment, "All right, young fellow, how about you praying for rain for us?" Embarrassed, and seeking an excuse, I said, "Where would I pray, here in the middle of the field?" And pointing to an old stump which they had plowed around, he said, "Right there; go over and kneel down on that stump and pray."

Timidly I walked over to the old stump that was about three feet across, crawled up on it, and knelt and prayed for rain. Within ten minutes a dark cloud rolled up, and it poured rain. Everyone ran for the barn and the hoeing was over for the day.

I've walked a long way since I knelt on the old stump to pray. God honored that prayer, but He has taught me so much since.

Prayer is not using God to get what we want. Prayer is partnership with God!

It may at first seem strange that in writing about conscience and ethics I should include a chapter on prayer; however, on further thought it becomes clear that in thinking of ethics we are immediately confronted with our inability to live up to the standard of righteousness by our own power. Prayer is an absolute necessity for righteous living, for only as we open our lives to God, and invite His work within us, can we practice the righteousness to which we are called (Romans 8:4).

Conscience, when informed, calls us to prayer, to acknowledge our need of God, and to enter into conversation with Him. One of the deeper aspects of guilt is an awareness that we ignore God rather than respond to Him. The thinking person will have a conscience on prayer. With Dr. Christopher Stendall I too pray, "Only one thing I ask of You, God, help me not to use my reason against the truth." An ancient Hebrew prayer expresses our need to be open to the truth:

> From the conscience that shrinks from new truth,
> From the laziness that is content with half-truth,
> From the arrogance that thinks it knows all truth,
> O God of truth, deliver us.

The Christian conscience will hold us accountable to exercise prayer as the expression of our covenant with God. We will recognize with Paul, "Our sufficiency is of God" (2 Corinthians 3:5). Jesus said, "Without Me you can do nothing" (John 15:4). Prayer is being thoughtfully honest. The psalms are marvelous expressions of prayer, exalting in the Lord, praising Him for His goodness (Psalms 111:1; 113:1-2; 130:1-4; 139:23-24).

PRAYER IS BEING HONEST

Prayer is the exciting venture of reaching out to God. It is responding to a personal God who is so near to us and yet so other! The educated conscience cries out, "O Thou who knowest me so utterly, help me to know Thee a little better today."

We cannot fully comprehend God, and yet we cannot but think about Him. To think is to be human. True, humanness is more than thought, but it always includes rationality. It is one of the more wonderful aspects of being human that we can think on God and think with God.

The wonder of God's grace is that He who is so totally other has come to us in Jesus Christ, the Son of Man. Meeting God in Jesus, we can think God-thoughts. A thinking person will be a praying person, for when we think deeply we become aware of our finitude and at the same time of our relation to God. Charles Wesley prayed, "Lord, unite the two so long disjoined, knowledge and vital piety."

Through the divine disclosure in "the Word, the Christ" and in "the Word written," we know God as the loving, gracious redeemer who in Christ invites us to come to Himself. As thinking persons we meet Him also in the silent Word expressed through His world. When we think on the design and purpose of creation, on the nature and depth of the human personality, we are led to think on God.

To see life whole, to sense the dynamic movement of the meanings that sustain life in spite of all evident perversions and exploitations, the thinking person is called to reach for the ultimate Meaning. When I pray, I am being honest about my place in this larger aspect of life, and I am committing myself to be responsible in life. It does not mean that I have all of the answers, but that I trust Him with answers. Augustine said: "For it is better for them to find You and leave the question unanswered, than to find the answer without finding You."[1]

Prayer is intellectual respect for God;
    it enables analysis and synthesis,
    it is the way to God's answers,
    it is the key to disciplined living.
Prayer is the development of God-consciousness;

it banishes paralyzing doubts,
it explains the reasons for our failures,
it moves one from the haphazard to God's order.

Moses met God as he stood before the bush that burned but was not consumed; as he sought the meaning of this phenomena which was beyond his perception of reality, he heard the voice of God addressing him. After offering numerous excuses, Moses yielded to God and became the leader of Israel. As we read his marvelous prayers, we are moved by his faith and the immediacy of his sharing with God (Exodus 33:12-20). The Apostle John writes, "The law was given through Moses; grace and truth came through Jesus Christ. No one has ever seen God, but God the only Son, who is at the Father's side, has made Him known" (John 1:17-18). In Christ we have both a new understanding of God and a new relation with God. We can now "think God" by "thinking Jesus." To think with Jesus means that we think with a new worldview, a new understanding of life and its basic relationships. Jesus' prayers were honest expressions of His relationship with the Father. In His prayers we discover how close He was to the Father, how intimate their relationship, and how honest He was about the enriching strength of His life being from the Father.

To think with Christ is to have a Christian worldview: to recognize a Creator distinct from creation, to realize that God has made us in His own image, to confess that sin is a perversion of the good, to experience reconciliation in Christ, to interpret life as redeemed, to walk in the Spirit, to share in the new community of the kingdom, and to serve as agents of His reconciliation in the world. Such prayer will be thought through carefully, so that what we ask of God will be consistent with the name of Christ, with a Christological worldview!

To pray is to think with God,
reaching out with our minds,
recognizing that God is there,
realizing that He accepts us,

reveling in His love,
responding in obedience.
To pray is to think and to act with God.

Dr. John Mackay once said, "Commitment without reflection is fanaticism in action, though reflection without commitment is the paralysis of all action!"

When His disciples asked Jesus to teach them to pray, He gave them, and us, the model prayer. "Our Father who art in heaven . . . " He does not let us say "My" Father over against other people's Father; nor "Their" Father, as though others are in another group; but "Our" Father, from which we understand the divine relationship as extended alike to all people. The prayers of Jesus call us to seek the Father's will above all else. Our one purpose in life is seeking and doing the will of God.

The Lord's Prayer as we know it becomes a model in humility, honesty, and hope. As a six-year-old lad I heard my great-grand-father, Bishop J.M. Shenk, pray this prayer in a poetic form at our lunch table, and I have never forgotten it:

Our Father in heaven, we hallow Thy name,
May Thy kingdom holy, on earth be the same;
Give to us daily, our portion of bread,
For 'tis from Thy bounty that all must be fed;
Forgive our transgressions, and keep us from sin;
For Thine is the kingdom, forever. Amen.

To pray is to identify with God, to take one's place in His world and work. To pray is to recognize that I am His, am in relation with Him. To pray is to participate as a steward, as a manager of His gifts of life and resources. To pray is to confess my dependency, to acknowledge my indebtedness. To pray is to be honest about not being autonomous.

In Mrs. Baillie's biographical note regarding her husband, the well-known churchman John Baillie, she refers to three things in his study which symbolized his career: the desk where he wrote, the chair where he read, and the pad where he knelt daily to pray! This is the balance between thinking by interacting with other minds and thinking in conversation with God.[2]

PRAYER IS BEING RESPONSIBLE

Accountability and *responsibility*—these two words express crucial aspects of being human. "No man is an island." We are a part of all whom we have met. As part of the human family we are accountable for our actions as to whether they are fair, just, compassionate, participatory for the well-being of others. Once we recognize accountability we will accept responsibility to order our lives in a manner which will execute decisions consistent with our role. Our conscience will not let us play games in prayer!

The reach of the mind beyond the known lets us be honest with the scientific and see that there is more than we control, that relating to the "Thou" is to be mastered.

To close the mind to the voice of God limits one to the conclusions of the laboratory, while the Lord stands at the door and knocks, awaiting our humble and honest admission.

When we say of a son or daughter, of a student or an employee, "That person is responsible," we mean that we have full trust in their integrity to make decisions and to function in a manner consistent with their character. God said this of Abraham, "I know him" (Genesis 18:19), speaking of His confidence in Abraham's character. God was simply saying that Abraham was a responsible person.

The prayer-dialogue that followed between Abraham and God is an expression of God's respect for, and Abraham's expression of, this responsibility. As Abraham prayed for God to spare Sodom, he must have had Lot and his family in mind. He continued his intercession until he asked God to spare Sodom for ten righteous persons. He had a right to expect ten, for Lot and his wife had daughters, evidently two married daughters for there is reference to sons-in-law, and two single daughters who left the city with Lot. Consequently, Lot and his wife and four daughters, who could each have had a person close to them also walking with God, would have made up ten righteous!

To pray intelligently is to be a responsible participant in God's kingdom. Prayer is not a magical exercise which takes care of issues for us without our needing to participate in the process of solution. Nor is prayer an exercise of "using" God as our servant, as a "cosmic bellhop" to fulfill our dreams without our partnership with Him. Dr. David Bosch, of South Africa, writes in his insightful manner:

> Too often we as missionaries use prayer as an escape from our responsibilities. We say so easily, when we have had a serious problem, "I have prayed about it, and now I leave it in God's hands." This appears to be very pious and submissive, but it may in fact be just a cover-up for our unwillingness to face realities. . . . Even in our most pious moments we remain sinners, prone to egoism. We then use our prayers merely as gimmicks to obtain divine sanction for our own blueprints. It is said that most accidents are due to egoism. The same is true of most prayer accidents.[3]

The secret of effective prayer is opening the center of our lives to Jesus Christ. As He always did the things that pleased the Father, so we should pray to know and to do God's will. When we learn to place things in God's hands, our intercessory prayers become quiet, confidential conversations with Him about persons we love. It is as though Jesus says, "I love these people even much more than you do; let us both pray them into the kingdom."

> God is present in all life with the influence of His omnipresent and almighty power, and no sphere of human life is conceivable in which religion does not maintain its demands, that God shall be praised, that God's ordinances shall be observed, and that every labor shall be permeated with fervent and ceaseless prayer. Wherever man may stand, whatever he may do, to whatever he may apply his

hand in agriculture, commerce, or industry, or his mind in the world of art and science, he is, in whatsoever it may be, constantly standing before the face of God.[4]

Prayer is a willing heart seeking to obey God. The biblical concept of obedience is the recognition that God is actually God in our lives. This is not to be legalism, but a relationship. Our sense of responsibility makes us stewards of our total life-experience. Not only do we belong to Him, but everything we are and have is His. Our stewardship does not begin with things; it begins with ourselves.

> Words in prayer raise our consciousness;
>   they are not to awaken God's consciousness,
>   but to bring our own consciousness to focus,
>   to direct it toward God.
> Whether there be words or not,
>   prayer is the attitude of humility,
>   the direction of one's spirit .toward God,
>   the expectation of God's engagement.

In concluding his first letter to the Thessalonians, Paul said that we are to "pray without ceasing" (5:16), or pray continuously. Just as two persons in a love-covenant sense what the other person thinks of a particular behavioral pattern, even without spoken words, so one who walks closely with God has a sense of His Word. As we interact with Him when we read His Word, we will responsibly seek an understanding of His will.

PRAYER IS PARTICIPATION WITH GOD

To pray is to engage one's self with God. What a fantastic experience, what a marvelous relationship—we can actually participate with God in the fulfillment of life! We are not only God's creation, but we are children in His family, participating in His gracious act of creating a people for Himself. God is not some distant Being whom we need to entreat, but our Father. The designation *Father* emphasizes not masculinity but the familial relationship. We come to Him as His children, for in Christ we have become children of God (John 1:12). "As a father has compassion on his children, so the Lord has compassion on them who fear Him" (Psalm 103:13). In this family, Jesus is not ashamed to call us brothers (Hebrews 2:11). In fact, He invites us to pray to the Father in His name. When we pray we are participating in the Father's work (Ephesians 3:14-19).

Bernard of Clairvaux outlined four steps of love. The first is to love oneself for one's own sake. The second is a movement from self-love to loving God for what God does for us. The third is the higher level, to love God for God's sake alone! And the fourth is full circle, to love ourselves and other human beings not for our sakes but for God's sake alone—because of who God is. Prayer is not self-suggestion; nor is it exhibitionism, lust for power, or rationalization.

Prayer is not merit but mercy; it is the sense of God's presence, the silence of hearing His words, the quest of His presence.

The high priestly prayer of our Savior is an expression of prayer as participation. This prayer shows us that Jesus extended the will of the Father in the world. When we pray in the name of Christ, this likewise is to be an extension of His will in the world. The words, "in Jesus name," are not a magical formula to be added to our requests, but are the directive for prayer. Everything the disciple does is because of the name, and is in the name, in full identity with Jesus.

Prayer is not overcoming God's reluctance; it is laying hold on God's willingness. God delights in doing good for humanity, because He created us for His glory. Evil is here because we ignore God, rebel at His will, and pervert life into selfish pursuits. Prayer is not overcoming something in God; it is overcoming our own egos, our own self-sufficiency, and autonomy. Our striving in prayer is to overcome those hindrances in us which keep us from identifying fully with the will of God.

The modern church must regain the sense of God's rule, the

understanding of the larger meaning of His will. We often ask
God to guide us in personal decisions—occupation, marriage
partner, living quarters—but fail to seek the understanding of
His will for society, for our nation, for our place in the global
village, for justice and peace. The New Testament calls us to a
Gospel of faith, not to the popular "success gospel."

> Jeremiah and Jesus placed their trust in the forsaking God!
> There was no longer a faith built upon God's obvious
> answer. They believed in God even though God did not
> answer! . . . Here we do not see an answer-theology. We
> see instead a relationship-theology.[5]

> So the church having lost its absolute—the kingdom of
> God—is now in a welter of conflicting relativisms, all bid-
> ding for the church's attention and loyalty. So the church
> leaves a blur instead of a mark. Where Paul could say,
> "This one thing I do," the church says, "these forty things I
> dabble in." The church needs nothing so much as it needs
> a rediscovery of the absolute, the absolute of the kingdom,
> that would bring life back into unity, point it to new goals,
> individual and collective, discover new power, the power
> of the Spirit, to move on to those goals, and give it nerve
> to face a hesitating and confused world.[6]

Above all, we come to God to know Him better! The marvelous expression of Paul's prayer for the Ephesians is the quest to
know the love of God in ways far beyond what we can experience intellectually. This wonderful fourfold expression of love in
Ephesians 3:14-19 is matched by John 3:16, the golden text of
the Bible:

> We know how wide God's love is—
> for God so loved the world.
> We know the length of His love—
> He gave His only Son.
> We know how deep love reaches—

that whoso comes to Him . . .
We know the height of His love —
should have eternal life!
(This can be sung to the tune of
"O Sacred Head, Now Wounded.")

PRAYER IS ENABLING GOD TO ACT

When we pray we release God's power! We do not determine
God's work, but we participate by extending His work through
our act of faith. God does not manipulate people, but stands
alongside in love awaiting our recognition and openness for Him
to act. Prayer is the exercise of our God-given freedom in which
we enable God to work without violating us.

The fact that our prayers give God freedom to act is clear
only if we think about God relationally. When a friend acknowledges your experience, knowledge, or wisdom in some area of
life, that acknowledgment frees you to share. Similarly, as we
prayerfully acknowledge the wisdom and guidance of God, He
becomes free to share further in our lives. God is love, and love
does not violate another. Love offers itself, and does so even at
tremendous cost. Love will share with another to the depth of
their problem, but will refuse to override or manipulate them.

In His love for us, God shares Himself totally. In Christ He
manifested this even to death on the cross. As I think of His
forgiving grace, I am awed by the fact that He will carry the
scars of his love forever! But His love does not manipulate us,
does not violate our freedom, does not coerce us. God waits to
act in our lives until we invite him to act, lest He violate our
freedom. Oh, yes, He brings convictions to induce us to recognize His will; He arranges circumstances to show us options; He
brings friends into our lives to encourage us in better choices,
but He awaits our move of faith.

True prayer is dedication, not demand;
it is a change of center,

69

> it is a journey from self to God.
> Prayer brings mental illumination,
> the guidance that comes from God
> as we pray, "Thy kingdom come."

When we pray we give God the moral freedom to act, to do the things He has wanted to do in our lives but has waited until we grant him permission. Prayer does move the hand of God, not in our entreating Him to move, but in our freeing Him to move, by opening ourselves to him.

There are innumerable things that God could do for this world if we would but honor Him with the respect that invites His actions. Jesus says that when we ask in His name He will do it, "so that the Son may bring glory to the Father"! (John 14:13) We should beware of the presumption that expects God to correct everything, whether we honor him or not. God is neither capricious nor irresponsible; He is holy love, a love that receives its character from His holiness.

If God will not violate the personality of His child, just as a wise parent does not violate the dignity of the child, it follows that God awaits our recognition, our faith, our reaching out to Him before He can move with integrity. The spirit that cries, "Help," is offering a prayer. This is evident in the words of the father who, desperate over the condition of his son, cried out, "Lord, I do believe; help me overcome my unbelief!" (Mark 9:24)

Discipleship is a life of active yieldedness to Christ, a relationship in which He empowers us for transformed living. We have entered the new order, for being in Christ we are new creatures. This is a spirituality of discipleship that includes:

- Our identity. We are new creatures "in Him."
- Our wholeness. We are unitary beings who do not separate the mind from emotions, behavior from belief, or serving Christ from walking in the Spirit of Christ.
- Our community. As part of His body, we belong to one another in worship and in discernment.
- Our attitudes. As we walk in the Spirit, we learn from the Master and identify with Him.

● Our devotion. We relate to the Lord in a fellowship of love. This means that we commune with Him and are in prayer-conversation with Him.

● Our standards. As disciples we come to His Word with our minds already made up to obey, because our behavior is the extension of our beliefs. Yet we do not put action above being.

● Our service. As disciples of Christ, we recognize that all of life is worship. We express our walk with Christ when we "give a cup of cold water" in His name.

As disciples we are enabled to act in the will of God by the empowering which comes from the risen Christ. In turn we enable Christ to do His work in and through us.

PRAYER IS AFFIRMING GOD'S SOVEREIGNTY

Prayer is the disciple's line of communication with the Master, the declaration that we are following Him. As one of our church deacons said in a retreat setting, "While I have surrendered my life to Christ, I need to keep the old self from pulling off a coup!" Another added, "The problem of being a living sacrifice is that such a sacrifice keeps crawling off of the altar." Prayer enables the divine/human relationship that continues to bring renewal of the mind (Romans 12:2).

Prayer lays its hand on the helm of the universe! God is in charge, but He moves *with* people rather than by overriding them. He is sovereign within Himself, controlled, not acting out of reaction but by the integrity of His purpose.

Sovereignty—what is it? Is it primarily authority? Does it mean basically that God is in charge? If He is in charge, why doesn't He correct the mess in the world? Is sovereignty to be seen as determinism? Does it mean that all that happens is somehow in God's will? Does it mean that God will overrule everything evil? If so, why are we not universalists? As to prayer, if God is sovereign and knows all that we need and will act accordingly, why pray? How does our concept of sovereignty avoid a consequent fatalism?

A careful definition of sovereignty will enable us to be more consistent in our thoughts about God. The highest attribute of divinity can be said to be His holiness, the attribute conditioning His love, extended to us in mercy while at the same time expressing justice. Sovereignty is God's holy inner integrity expressed as self-determination. God can express these attributes of love, justice, mercy, and sovereignty, because of who He is, because of His holiness that includes wholeness, His total self-determination. He is sovereign, acting from Himself, not in reaction to us.

> That God is sovereign is my security.
> He can be depended on,
> He will be true to himself,
> He is self-determined,
> He is patient,
> He will always be love and loving.

God's sovereignty is His own inner control. He is self-controlled and does not act capriciously. He does not break in upon our lives and manipulate or dominate us. God is self-determined, saying, "I will have mercy on whom I will have mercy" (Exodus 33:19), meaning that He decides within Himself as to His expressions of mercy and compassion. God's sovereignty is our security, the assurance of our freedom to be persons who, created in His image, have the freedom to respond to Him in faith or to negate Him in selfishness. What a fantastic God! He is secure, sovereign, not threatened by our freedom nor so insecure as to authoritatively determine our relationship.

Prayer is the mind "stayed on God," seeking God first, "searching with all the heart." One does not become an artist, a pianist, or physician, unless concentrating on subject matter, being intent upon life's quest. We must concentrate on knowing God, on sharing fellowship with Him, being excited about each interchange.

In his book *No Handles on the Cross*, Koyoma shows us that when we come to the sovereign Lord, we agree that He is in charge, when we take up the cross, we accept His right to apportion to us our role of service for him. A.W. Tozer once said, "The person who carries a cross no longer determines his own destiny."

For the disciple, prayer includes entering covenant for renewal of the vitality of our relation with the sovereign God. But when we speak of spiritual renewal we raise issue of the many forms or expressions of spirituality. Let me list several.

• Pietistic spirituality carries a strong emphasis on the devotional life, the "quiet time," and corresponding behavior.

• Revivalistic spirituality, such as characterized the Great Awakenings, East Africa Revival, and Keswick Conventions, emphasizes repentance as a continuous spirit of life.

• Contemplative spirituality, such as the emphasis of Thomas Merton and many retreat centers, calls us to the inward and upward aspects of meditation and response.

• Charismatic spirituality, with the many theological strains in the movement, is a call for us to enter into the subjective aspects of faith, to participate in our role of appropriation.

• Liturgical spirituality, the application of the meaning of religious symbols, something which I call "artology," engages us in renewal by symbols which call us to meaning.

• Holistic spirituality emphasizes the community aspects of spiritual enrichment, especially recognizing feminist spirituality as adding the intuitive and relational dimensions to the more traditional perceptive and active emphases, a wholeness which calls for us to think of empowering one another in the body of Christ.

• Relational spirituality understands the psychological aspects of interpersonal relations and emphasizes freedom and fellowship, the freedom for self-actualization in a caring community of love.

• Holiness spirituality in the Wesleyan tradition calls us to experience a total surrender of our selves to the rule of the sovereign Spirit.

• Discipleship spirituality is an emphasis on walking with Jesus on the way; it is a following of Him in participation, an active yieldedness to His rule. As Hans Denck, an Anabaptist of the sixteenth-century, said, "No one knows Christ truly unless he follows Him daily in life."

PRAYER IS IDENTIFYING THE DIVINE WILL

The way of peace is to live in the will of God. To seek His will and to do it is life's highest calling. "Our chief end is to glorify God and to enjoy Him forever." Prayer is opening oneself to God, to His presence and to His will. His will is seen fully in Jesus the Christ, in His life as well as His teachings and His deeds. Therefore, we need to meet Jesus in the Word.

It is very meaningful and enriching to pray over the Scripture. When we pray as we read the Bible, His written Word comes alive in us. We should actually talk with Him as we read, with expressions such as, "Yes, but," and "So what?" and "That is what I want." Above all, we must read the Bible seeking to understand God and His will.

The greatest answer to prayer is our experience of the presence of God Himself. In teaching the disciples to pray, Jesus said, "If you then, though you are evil, know how to give good gifts to your children, how much more will your Father in heaven give the Holy Spirit to those who ask Him!" (Luke 11:13) The Holy Spirit is God present; as Jesus said, "God is spirit, and His worshipers must worship in spirit and in truth" (John 4:24). Paul wrote to the Ephesians, "Be filled with the Spirit," using the present imperative form, meaning that we are commanded to be continually filled with the Spirit (Ephesians 5:18). There is no greater answer to prayer than to share the joy of the presence of the Holy Spirit.

Richard of Chichester, a saint of the thirteenth century, expressed himself in this prayer:

> Day by day, dear Lord,
> Of Thee three things I pray;
> To see Thee more clearly,

Love Thee more dearly,
Follow Thee more nearly,
Day by day.

Seeking God's will involves careful study of the Scripture, but it should also include sharing with a covenant group of believers who will help each other test interpretations and judgments. Seeking God's will involves prayer in which one surrenders to the sovereign will of the Spirit and waits to sense the Spirit's witness or inner confirmation. When a group holds us accountable to honestly and unselfishly search for the Lord's will, they provide an invaluable service. When they share the weight of the decision, they are exercising the Lord's word that His disciples are to participate in the "binding" and "loosing" process.

I shall long remember the relief and joy in the face of a young woman who was making a major and difficult decision regarding the will of God about marrying a person whose past held some situations well outside of the will of God, when I invited her to bring her friend and meet with the elders and let us work through this with her. Our act of binding and loosing provided her the confirmation of God's will and released her from being so alone in the process. Community is a covenant of solidarity in which together we act as one.

Just as Jesus lived in solidarity with humanity, and just as He as the risen Lord continues this solidarity with us, so we are to share solidarity with the human family. This awareness enables us to see each one as created in the image of God, and to recognize, be they poor or rich, illiterate or educated, unrefined or sophisticated, that they like us are equal recipients of God's grace.

Praying in the will of God does not mean only finding His will for personal life, what occupation, where to live, who to marry, how to make an important decision; it also means discovering God's will and purpose for great social issues of life. What is God's will for the church on major sociopolitical issues, human rights, justice issues, apartheid, the problems of the poor, racial and sexual prejudices, family issues from divorce to abortion, peacemaking in a world of violence, world mission that transcends the national enemies of one's country, attitudes and policies of the church in matters where international conflict affects the integrity of the church as a part of the global family of God's people? Praying in the will of God is participating in God's mission and purpose for the world.

PRAYER IS BEING ANOTHER'S DEFENSE

What does it mean to intercede, to pray for another? Jesus once said to Peter, "Satan has asked to sift you as wheat. But I have prayed for you, Simon, that your faith may not fail. And when you have turned back, strengthen your brothers" (Luke 22:31). How do we pray for another? How do we intercede? By interceding, I mean praying in effective and informed identification with the person, not just saying, "Bless Henry and Mary and . . . " What does it mean to enter into another's struggles and resist the evil with them? What are the dynamics of interchange between the divine and the demonic that are so intense that Paul says "the Spirit Himself intercedes for us with groans that words cannot express"? (Romans 8:26)

One of the amazing stories in the Book of Acts is that of Peter's deliverance from prison the night before he was to have been martyred by King Herod (Acts 12:1-19). Herod had just killed James the Apostle, and there was every reason to believe that he would kill Peter as planned. The passage tells us, "So Peter was kept in prison, but the church was earnestly praying to God for him" (verse 5). We cannot be sure that they were praying for his release; they may have been praying for his courage and faithfulness. They, of course, knew that once before under temptation he had denied his Lord, and they may well have been praying for his faithfulness.

However, God, who has a way of doing "immeasurably more than all we ask or imagine" (Ephesians 3:20), sent an angel to negotiate the miraculous escape from the prison cell where Peter had been bound and guarded with four squads of soldiers of four members each. When Peter arrived at the home of the mother of John Mark, sister to Barnabas, and interrupted their prayer meeting, they were dumbfounded with unbelief until his presence convinced them of his escape. This story is a wonderful account of a group of believers in intercessory prayer, and of God answering beyond their expectations.

Prayer for others is not only intercession for their physical freedom; it also includes intercession for their liberation emotionally, socially, materially, and spiritually. John writes that if anyone sees a brother "commit a sin that does not lead to death, he should ask and God will give him life" (1 John 5:17). It is not so much that we must understand fully the nature of God's holy integrity in His dealing with the satanic, as that we know that He accepts and hears our prayers of identification with another who is in need.

Often ours will be thought-prayers expressing our consciousness of others' problems, of their needs, and we will enter with them into the quest for deliverance or victory. Our prayers may be to help them come to the consciousness of need, of the nature of the sin or perversion that is destroying life. A thinking person who becomes involved in sin goes through an extensive rationalization, and we need to help them come to the consciousness of their compromise and of God's claim on their lives.

> Consciousness is to be truly a self
> reviewing memories of one's past,
> anticipating the future,
> and thinking realistically on the present.
> Prayer-consciousness is Christian hope:
> faith that reaches out to God,
> love that embraces others,
> and joy that liberates one's soul.

As in a court of law where Satan is the accuser of the brother, so we can be a witness for the defense, not to seek to clear the brother but to pursue the freedom in which one can say yes to God. As Job prayed for his friends, as Abraham prayed for Lot, as Samuel was a friend who prayed for Saul, and especially as Paul prayed for the host of men and women named in his epistles, so we are to pray for, identify with, and engage spiritual resources on behalf of others (Colossians 1:9-13).

Intercession means to identify with another in spiritual empathy, to stand with them in their trial, even in their despair or weakness. In some very difficult circumstances, Esther and I have found that the intercessory prayers of persons in the congregation have provided us a rich emotional and spiritual lift. When we intercede we literally place our hand in the face of the devil and say, "Stand back, our God is moving in here." Our brother or sister may be too discouraged to ask it clearly or intelligently, but we join in the prayer and provide a freedom for God to act.

The ambassador from Britain, confronting the head of government in Turkey, when the Armenian people were being massacred, said, "My Queen will not stand silent and watch this people be exterminated." So we, by prayer for others, are declaring to Satan, "My King will not stand silent and let this life be destroyed!"

> A priest at another's elbow means
> support in times of weakness,
> partnership of strength,
> communion with God together,
> a ministry of caring, of understanding.

Intercession is confrontational; it is daring to delineate and to defy evil. It not only defies some mystical evil power, but it confronts evil in society and in the lives of those who are special to us. If the problem is alcoholism, the family or circle of caring people have a lot to do with confronting and supporting the person who is being liberated. The same may be said for many problems, such as drugs, overeating, and sexual perversions or addictions. Intercession is to put one hand in God's and the other in the hand of a friend, and draw the two together.

Intercession is joining with others in the spiritual conquest. It is not talking God into doing something, but is participating with God's action as He, with and through us, continues to invade this world. Jesus said, "On this rock I will build my church, and the gates of Hades will not overcome it" (Matthew 16:18). Intercession means that we join with Christ in the engagement of the conquest for the kingdom of heaven.

PRAYER IS WITHSTANDING EVIL

We have been redeemed! We live in the victory of Christ. We have been recreated in the new life provided in Christ. Even though Satan continues to usurp authority in the lives of those on whom God has His claim, we are to stand "in the liberty wherewith Christ has made us free" (Galatians 5:1). It is our security in Christ, being sealed with the Holy Spirit, that enables us to withstand the evil one.

True, we live in a fallen world, but we also live in a redeemed world; we must boldly affirm that we stand in the victory of Christ. We have been reconciled, restored, and released to do the will of God. Yet in genuine faith we are to be honest about the fact that we are not the victors; Christ is victor, and we share that victory through which we confront the evil. In Him we can resist the devil and he will flee, as James says (4:7-10).

Prayer is our declaration that we do not surrender. Prayer is the flag of faith over the residence of the child of God. Prayer is the declaration to the opponent that we are in touch with the resources of the divine! A failure to pray signals that we have given up hope. But we are saved by hope, the dauntless conviction that Christ is victor (Romans 8:24).

When Jesus referred to His disciples as salt of the earth and light of the world, He was declaring that we are a transforming influence amidst evil. The light is to keep shining in the darkness. No matter how small the light, no amount of darkness is able to hide it. Prayer is such a light, for prayer is evidence that God has partners in the world, it is the signal of our commonality with God.

> God is "the soul's imperative necessity,"
> the fulfillment of our reason for existence,
> the source of life and of insight,
> the awakening of new capacities.
> Without God we plod life's dusty road,
> amass amazing information,
> make observations one upon another,
> and miss the heart of life!

The first and best thing that we can do about life's problems is to pray. Prayer acknowledges our primary relation to God. Faced with problems in the political and social order, we are instructed first of all to pray for those in authority (1 Timothy 2:1-4). In this text Paul emphasizes that the ultimate concern is that all persons come to repentance and to the knowledge of God in Jesus Christ. We drive back the darkness by sharing the light! We overcome evil by doing good (Romans 12:21). We change the world by sharing the gospel of Christ so clearly and effectively that people are called to become disciples of Jesus Christ (Matthew 28:19-20).

James tells us to "resist the devil" and he will flee from us because of our identification with Christ. While Satan did his worst to destroy Christ by crushing our Lord's body, he couldn't crush His spirit. Christ's victory on the cross and His resurrection have rendered Satan his defeat, and we stand in this victory. We overcome the devil not by a new battle but by standing in the victory of Christ. He has won! So we have won! "They overcame him by the blood of the Lamb and by the word of their testimony" (Revelation 12:11).

Evil in itself is self-defeating; it exists as a parasite, as a moocher, for evil can have appeal only by falsely identifying with something that is good, even while it perverts the good. God ultimately overcomes evil not by exercising His superior power, but by expressing His superior quality. When God withdraws everything good—light, love, peace, joy, friendship, kindness, pleasure—there will be nothing left that has any goodness in it . . . and that is hell! Satan will be bound by the simple act of God withdrawing everything that is good and leaving evil to itself; there will be nothing left but hell.

Overcoming and withstanding evil is not to meet evil on its own ground and thereby cheapen our approach. Rather, we overcome evil by bringing God and His goodness into every situation, evidencing the values of the spiritual qualities of life. Our prayers are to equip us to penetrate all of life with the holy.

In our conversations with God, we declare our identification with Him. This identification is to be far more prominent than our past identification with sin. As Paul says, "We have taken off the old self with its practices and have put on the new self, which is being renewed in knowledge in the image of its Creator" (Colossians 3:9-10). We are in His family.

PRAYER IS SOLIDARITY WITH CHRIST

For us to say with Thomas, "My Lord, and my God," is to enter into solidarity with Christ. The nature of discipleship is full identification with Christ. We are His servants, His disciples, His inheritance. We belong to Him.

Prayer is our declaration to Jesus that He is Lord in actuality, that we are His servants in reality. Prayer becomes the heart cry of the person of faith, not for blessings from God but for God Himself! "As the deer pants for streams of water, so my soul pants for You, O God" (Psalm 42:1). Life is not in self-fulfillment, but finding oneself in God, loving God, and being loved by God.

Paul's phrase "in Christ" is, therefore, the full sum of the believer's identity. As disciples of Jesus Christ we follow Him, we worship Him, we talk with Him, we obey Him, we walk with Him. In prayer for the Colossians, Paul asked for their maturity in Christ (Colossians 1:28-2:3). It is especially significant that Paul, not having seen the Colossians in the flesh, speaks of how he exerted himself for them in prayer.

As Christians we too often identify with our religion more than with Christ, have faith in our faith rather than in our Lord, identify with our denominational cause more than with the dynamic life of the Spirit. Without solidarity with Christ, all of the good that can be found in other identities is empty. We are first and foremost disciples of Christ, and we cannot meaningfully walk with Him without emotional, intellectual, and relational solidarity with Him.

In John 15, Jesus shows us that we bear fruit because we abide in Him. The only branch that bears fruit is the one that abides in the vine. And the fruit always appears on the new growth! The branch itself is involved in the process of transmitting nourishment. David Bosch says, "A channel remains unaffected by what flows through it, but a branch has, first of all, to absorb the nutritive power which comes to it from the roots and trunk. It has to make all this a part of itself, and allow itself to be affected and renewed and transformed by that power."[7]

What makes a difference in the world is not our claim to perfection but our declaration of identification with Christ. Evidence that this is not pretense but practice is in the solidarity expressed in mature prayer. Sharing with and for one another in prayer creates the unity of the body, in spirit and in life.

Our congregation in Washington, D.C. is guided by a board of elders. Our pastoral team of three is part of the board as teaching elders, but we function as a distinct unit of elders. We meet every other week for prayer, and the alternate weeks for prayer followed by a work session. It is in prayer together that we have found the unity of the Spirit and harmony in our service for Christ. Another group, the intercessors, meet weekly for an hour of prayer for the congregation. What we are learning is that time with God in prayer is some of the more important time for our community enrichment.

In the early church we see a good example of the pattern of praise and solidarity in prayer. Upon the release of Peter and John following their arrest by the Sanhedrin, they joined the congregation in prayer. "Sovereign Lord . . . You made the heaven and the earth and the sea, and everything in them. You spoke by the Holy Spirit through the mouth of Your servant, our father David." Following a quotation from the psalms they recited briefly the history of Christ's work, and then made their petition for boldness to be faithful witnesses. "After they prayed, the place where they were meeting was shaken. And they were all filled with the Holy Spirit and spoke the word of God boldly" (Acts 4:31).

Our prayers are not limited petitions but expressions that honor the greatness and the majesty of our God.

> We are coming to a King,
> worthy petitions we should bring!
> for His grace and power are such
> none can ever ask too much.

PRAYER IS SOLIDARITY WITH THE BODY

The better illustration of the church is a symphony, not a solo, for in a symphony each player masters an instrument so that the group can do together what no one individual could do alone.

The body of Christ is ONE, but it has many parts, made up of individuals who identify with Christ (1 Corinthians 12:12-13). While the Spirit unites us together in prayer, our solidarity with Christ is extended to become solidarity with one another (Philippians 1:3-7).

This solidarity with one another as disciples, when expressed within a congregation, between congregations, between denominations, or across the national lines in the global community, can change the world. Such prayer can remove the gulf between the races, between the haves and the have-nots, between the developed and developing worlds, and can help correct the aparthied, terrorism, and wars which plague our world.

The church is a network of faith in the global community. But the "Christian" West has been so individualistic that we find it almost impossible to enter into community. Only in Christ can we become one body, and in Him all confess one Lord. As we take our place in His body, we can take our place in His world. The praying Christian will be frontally involved in

83

the rights of all humans to live with freedom, with justice, and with love. Our solidarity with Christ brings us into solidarity with His mission, which means solidarity with His people, all of them!

> To share in intercession for another,
>> is reaching out in love,
>> is affirming the other beyond oneself,
>> is actualizing our oneness in Christ.
> To intercede is to be in community;
>> it is inviting God to intervene,
>> it is enjoining the other to be open to God,
>> it is anticipating the Spirit's creative presence.

Community as a dynamic of the Spirit is a fellowship of trust, in which we trust ourselves to one another. This is the risk of faith, not only faith in God but faith in the people of God. I have just been enriched by a meeting of the deacons of our congregation. The convener of the deacons, Phyllis Miller, arranged to have one of the very effective members of the congregation, Kathy Gathro, address the group on the spiritual qualities of leadership. She challenged us to joy and freedom in the Spirit by a leadership that comes not from our strengths but from leading with our weaknesses.

Kathy's insights spoke to all of us, but in an especially meaningful way to me. When we lead from our strengths we tend to hide behind them. People don't really get to know us; they admire our strengths but are not drawn to us. We must become willing to be vulnerable, put our strengths in check, move in the faith that will let us lead from our weaknesses, so that the Spirit may be dominant. In turn, we grow by needing to work with and from our weaknesses, even though in doing so we become vulnerable. Servant leadership is God's way for us to enable others.

As we share in the openness of mutual service, our prayers can be the experience of a spiritual consensus, an "agreeing as touching anything" so that we may by faith ask in the name of Christ. As we pray together we can unselfishly ask God for the wisdom and the filling of the Holy Spirit needed in the group, not asking individualistically but for the body, asking personally but asking especially for the community of disciples. We never grow spiritually at the expense of others; we grow best as we take others along.

The church, or congregation, has become the temple of the Holy Spirit who dwells with us (1 Corinthians 3:17). Here Paul says that "if anyone destroys God's temple God will destroy him;" a literal translation of the Greek reading is, "God will wreck the church-wrecker." In 1 Corinthians 6, Paul says that our individual persons become the dwelling place of the Holy Spirit (6:19), but in chapter 3, he is speaking of the unity of the community of believers.

Prayer unifies us with one another, for when we meet in the presence of Christ, trivial things that divide us are seen as unimportant, and the great realities of our faith bind us in common fellowship. Our oneness or sense of community is experienced by relating to each other in and through Jesus Christ our Lord. Our unity is in Him.

Prayer is opening oneself to God; it is meeting God in surrender and in the obedience of faith. To think Christianly about life is to see prayer as identification with God in the fulfillment of life. It is in prayer that the largest meanings of life become our own, for prayer is receiving from God the enrichment of His grace.

The story is told of John Wesley preaching in an evil section of London where ribald sensuality was prevalent. Two ruffians appeared at the edge of the crowd and asked roughly, "Who is this preacher? What right has he to spoil our fun? We'll show him." In a moment they were elbowing their way through the crowd, each with a stone in his hand. But just as they were ready to let fly at Wesley's face, he began speaking about the power of Christ to change the lives of sinful people. While he spoke, a serene beauty spread over his face.

As the two youths stood there with their arms poised in midair, one turned to the other, "He ain't a man, Bill, he ain't a man." Their arms came down, and Wesley finished his sermon.

As he passed through the crowd, he came near where the two young men were standing. One of them reached out and almost tenderly touched Wesley's coat. Wesley paused, placed his hands on the heads of the two young men and said, "God bless you, my boys!" When he moved on, one ruffian said to the other, "He is a man, Bill; he's a man like God!"

5. CONSCIENCE AND EDUCATION

The Christ-shaped conscience results from an honest and informed understanding of the person and life of Christ. He is our norm for ethics. It is often painful to go through the adjustments of harmonizing one's conscience with the Word and will of Christ. Jesus confronted a deeply held conviction of people in His day and asked them to accept change. Answering the Pharisees who criticized His disciples for picking some heads of grain on the Sabbath, He said, "The Sabbath was made for man, not man for the Sabbath. So the Son of Man is Lord even of the Sabbath" (Mark 2:27-28).

This text always brings back an experience I had when I was a young man of nineteen. It was summertime, between semesters at college, and I was working in western Ohio in my home community, and sharing in the life of the church. Our congregation, Pike Mennonite Church, was interested in beginning a mission program in the Allegheny Mountains of Kentucky. I was one of a carload of men who made a trip down for a few days in the "hollers" to enjoy the hospitality of the mountain people, live in their homes, and establish both friendship and understanding of our mission. Our trip involved a Sunday, and at noon the men stopped in a town and went into the restaurant for lunch. Since I had something of a conscience against buying on a Sunday, I excused myself and remained alone in the auto. When they returned, one of the men quoted the above text to me and began to interpret it to call me to a new freedom. And step by step I began to understand how one's conscience may be conditioned by past impressions more than by correctly interpreting the Word. I still have a conscience against unnecessary spending on Sunday, but I have been set free from legalistic restraint.

Careful and clear thinking is necessary for an informed conscience, for the development of conviction for high levels of morality. The goal is that we will think "Christianly." Christian scholarship is an intellectual discipline that interfaces faith with fact, reason with revelation, and love with life with the openness of search for the understanding of truth in every area. In no way is the Christian scholar less rigorous, less academic, less scientific, or less open in the search to understand truth and reality than the secular scholar.

The Christian thinker is honest about the presence of presuppositions of faith in his or her life and thought, and in turn asks the secular thinker to be just as honest about presuppositions in research or thought exercises.

It seems to me that a case might well be made that the human personality and mind by its nature always seeks for an identity with ultimate reality. With this premise the Christian thinker who affirms that the Ultimate Reality is God, and consequently does not seek this Reality elsewhere, may be more objective than the secular thinker. The latter may actually tend toward deification of areas of research as though one such area may become Ultimate Reality. Consequently, the researcher may lose a degree of objectivity.

The fact that there remains mystery in our knowledge of God calls us to humility before truth, to reverent, rigorous, self-critical thought. Theologies or philosophies which primarily address human experience, cultural concern, sociological analysis, humanistic ideologies each tend, consciously or unconsciously, to put man at the center and to create a god on our own terms. To think Christianly is to think with openness to God and His

Truth in all areas, seeking to understand and to interface truths in harmony with the whole without doing violence to any of the particular truths.

It is a strange premise which we offer to secular minds: a God beyond us who comes to us and seeks us out, human beings focused on a point beyond themselves, new dimensions of life found within the Scriptures, and the God who confronts us in His Word.

In order to relate this faith premise to the processes of informed thought and conscience, there are patterns necessary to the thinking disciple.

• A disciple is one who identifies personally with Jesus Christ, who lives in solidarity with Christ, who lives out this relationship with Christ, and who serves in the spirit of Christ.

• A disciple engages both reason and faith, understanding faith as a rational exercise, in that faith is response to evidence and reason is the function of examining and clarifying the evidence.

• A disciple comes to the issues of life with the decision already made to answer them with the integrity of solidarity with Christ and the resultant freedom from self-centered manipulation.

• A disciple is one who in having come to Christ experiences God's transforming grace, enjoying in this change a new freedom in which the mind is liberated to think with God-discernment, to focus on such ethical elements as equity, justice, love, and peace, as well as on the redemptive dimensions of grace.

• A disciple, while living in a fallen world, finds his or her primary frame of reference to be the "redeemed community" in which a "community hermeneutic" is exercised, challenging and testing the assumptions of the individual mind.

• A disciple comes to the Scripture with the decision already made to obey it, once the will of God is understood, and then engages scholarship with a commitment to obey Truth, while testing his or her understanding of Truth. This is to recognize that what each of us believes is not necessarily what the Scripture says, but what we understand the Scripture to say.

• A disciple is open to the Holy Spirit for His special gifts of insight, and enduement, and to the fruit of the Spirit as God's grace for effective expressions of love as we serve others.

As I look at these characteristics of a thinking disciple, I do not find in them elements that of themselves should alter or in any way limit the exercises of the mind in research, analysis, creative work, or academic excellence. Rather these are the very expressions of character which make for honest, objective, and diligent scholarship that we all respect.

THINKING CLEARLY

To exercise the mind simply for the routine functions of living is to make of the mind a computer programmed by the routine necessities of life. To open one's mind to the mystery beyond us is the beginning of in-depth thinking. It is in this exercise of thought that we participate in the grandeur of humanness! As we develop convictions, we become persons of moral integrity.

As a student I once prefaced a question to my philosophy professor by saying, "I'm sure you've thought about this, and I want to ask . . . " to which he responded, "I've done more thinking than anything else I've done in life!" This Christian man has distinguished himself as an outstanding thinker and writer in philosophy and ethics. He is a model of the fact that serious thinking is an exacting exercise, a demanding discipline.

A basic difference between us as people is in how we think, how much we think, and how authentically we think. We refer to clear thinking and to fuzzy thinking. In far too many cases, what we call thinking is simply rearranging our ideas or prejudices. To clarify ideals and to inform our consciences, we need to think intentionally.

We sometimes speak of thinking deeply, and what we mean is to think beyond the surface, beyond the status quo, beyond the phenomenon to cause or root meaning. Such thinking is not necessarily synonymous with education, for in too many cases the thought processes in academia are in themselves identified with the academic status quo. It has been suggested that only about five percent of the people think conceptually, about fifteen percent think about concrete things, and the other eighty percent simply rearrange their prejudices and call it thinking!

Christian thinkers need to rigorously pursue the disciplines of scholarship. In fact, we should be asking the more serious questions of epistemology, interpreting intelligently the relation between reason and revelation, reason and faith, reason and conscience, perception and meaningful relationships. Life is not just ideas, but is actualizing our perceptions and relationships in love, justice, and freedom. Christian thinkers are realists about the relation between thought and conscience.

It is frequently implied that liberals think and conservatives do not. This suggestion is itself an indication of shallow or biased thinking. A liberal may fail to think profoundly by simply echoing a status quo thought pattern of a "liberal" nature, or by simply reacting to a conservative thought pattern and thereby appearing to be avant-garde.

On the other hand, a conservative is often regarded as a nonthinking person because he perpetuates values of the past. While this *may* be true it does not necessarily follow, for a genuine conservative must do some careful thinking to bring yesterday's values into today's thought and life and make them understood. Scholarly thought is not the private domain of either liberal or conservative. The thinking of both would be enhanced by honest engagement of one another.

EPISTEMOLOGY

One of the unique aspects of being created in the image of God is our ability to think rationally. This involves the process of thought, the rational or logical relationship of our perception of concepts, and the science of acquiring knowledge. Epistemology is the science of knowing; it is the method of arranging perceptions into consistent, understandable and communicable bits of knowledge.

91

Education is an act of faith, for in the passing of cultural values and insights from one generation to another, we express an implied faith that we are selecting essential meanings that we have found to be important. In turn the recipient or learner is acting in faith that what is being taught can be assimilated into his or her thought processes as a valid and important transmission of values.

The acquiring of knowledge in any field, including new discoveries by scientific research, is inextricably bound to history. We build on insights or stimuli which come to us reexpressed as a new synthesis or discovery. But these developments are not in isolation from the stimulus and insights that have been tested earlier. Of his research in his quest to develop the electric light, Thomas Edison commented that he had not failed, he had simply identified 10,000 ways that didn't work!

Learning viewed holistically calls us to recognize that obedience itself is a way of knowing.[1] Some areas of knowledge are directly related to doing and are what we call "skill courses." Examples include instruction in learning to ride a bicycle or fly a plane, training to become a public speaker or an artist. We follow a similar pattern in learning to pray, to trust God, to live in His will.

REASON AND REVELATION

Reason does not preclude revelation, nor does divine revelation exclude reason. Revelation is God's self-disclosure, the unfolding of the knowledge of Himself in history. In social relationships, we truly know one another only when we each open up and reveal ourselves to each other. The knowledge of God, the One wholly other, is dependent upon God's self-disclosure, His revealing himself to us. The fact that He did this in history, supremely in Jesus Christ, means that we can test the claims and understand the disclosure and message, always moving beyond the Word written to the Word of whom the Bible speaks.

The relationship of reason and faith is central to our understanding of the divine self-disclosure. Faith is reasonable or logical in that faith is responsive to evidence. Faith is not a blind wish, but is a rational response to reasons for belief or nonbelief. Actually, nonbelief in God is also a faith, for one cannot prove no God any more than one can prove a God.

As we look at the relation of faith and reason, there are four premises usually stated on this issue.

Reason is primary and excludes faith.
Reason is primary and includes faith.
Faith is primary and excludes reason.
Faith is primary and includes reason.

Christians generally hold to either the second or the fourth of these, differing on perceptions of this paradox of epistemology, but agreeing that reason and faith must be held together. As Anselm said of the believer, "Faith seeks understanding," so we would see him agreeing more with the fourth premise. On the other hand, Descartes said, "I think, therefore I am," appearing to put number one as primary, possibly number two. As we engage the interfacing of reason and faith my conclusion is that they are each dependent on the other, that like two sides of a cogwheel, they interlock and are mutually dependent.

Should we see reason and revelation as standing over against one another, we would be implying that knowledge never comes to us from beyond ourselves. Revelation is a divine disclosure that breaks in upon our consciousness, but it is not irrational. The perception of revelation in concepts, in art, in music, in science, is not without rational perception or function in the expression of such meaning. To imply that thinking about God is less an exercise of the normal reason than thinking about the dynamics of relational realities such as justice, freedom, love, courage, morality, and so on, is to misunderstand the function of reason.

In all honesty we must say that we cannot prove God, nor can we prove that God is not! Faith that there is a God and the alternative faith that there is no God, must be seen alike as expressions of a faith that reflects the way in which we look at the evidence. A friend of mine in Washington, D.C., Burnett Thompson, agreed to meet regularly with a group of agnostics to talk about ultimate meanings, without any mention of God. But from the first session it was the agnostics who found it impossible to avoid reference to God! One of the primary values of dialogue between the Christian and the non-Christian is that it calls us each to think carefully about the evidence, and about our interpretation of the evidence. A reasoned faith is the function of the secure mind.

SECULAR AND CHRISTIAN THOUGHT

There is a myth in our society that the secular is the broad realm and the spiritual or sacred is a narrow realm. Actually it is the other way around. Georgia Harkness has said of secularism, "It is the orientation of life around humanity as though God does not exist." Often called a "theological maverick," Bishop Pike defined secularism as "this-is-all-there-is-ism" or again as "there-ain't-any-more-ism." The spiritual or sacred permeates the secular, just as in Christ, "the Word became flesh and lived for a while among us" (John 1:14). Christian thinking can engage all of the secular, and in addition seeks to engage all of the realm of the spiritual.

An old story about Dr. Mortimer Adler illustrates this. Following a dinner one evening, as the guests relaxed in conversation in the living room, the discussion went against Adler's position and he got up in a huff and slammed through a door. In the silence that followed someone wanted to relieve the embarrassment of the hostess and said, "Well, he's gone," to which she replied, "No, he isn't; that's a closet." When we slam a door to leave God's presence, we do not enter a larger world but rather we enter the closet of "this-is-all-there-is-ism."

The process of secularization is in many ways a direct result of the developments of humanness enhanced by the Christian faith, and is thereby the consequence of humanity seeking to fulfill intelligent and creative qualities of our created humanness as being in God's likeness. The tragedy is when people make a religion of secularism. Our mission as Christian thinkers is not to deny the value of secularization but to seek the hallowing of all of life, the interfacing of the sacred and the secular, and the informing of our own consciences but also the conscience of society.

MEANING AND VALUES

To speak of intrinsic worth raises the issue of meaning in life. When we think deeply about meaning we are led to distinguish between symbol and reality, to move from the phenomenological to the real which is beyond, but read through, appearance. As we look at that which we say is real, we move to establish some hierarchy of value.

Not all things that we say are real are of the same value. As in the monetary exchange, a one-dollar bill is tender as authentic as the fifty-dollar bill, but it does not have the same value. So in life, various experiences or perceptions may be equally authentic but not of the same value. As thinking people, we evaluate and select, and those selections make basic differences in our lifestyles.

Much is said today about the importance of values, especially of Judeo-Christian values. But what is meant by this term? Even with this as a basic value premise, is there clarity among us on such things as the supreme value of the human person, of life, of the value of freedom, and of justice? Is faith, as expressed in this value system, an integrating force in the thinking person's life, recognized as important for our social welfare as well as for our spiritual well being? And do we have common understandings of the place of love in human equity and opportunity, of what it means to love one's neighbor as one's self? Basic to each of these is the value of personal openness to God, to the One beyond ourselves who calls us by name and gives us our identity in relationship with Him and with the redeemed community.

Unfortunately, we speak of values and of values education with no clear understanding of what those values are and of how they are to be achieved. An emphasis on values should mean that we place the issue of ethics in the forefront, for values have to do with ethics, with right and wrong, with the good and the better, with value judgments. For the Christian, the highest expression of values is seen in the person of Christ, "who did always those things that pleased the Father." This premise calls us to both think and to behave Christologically. That is to say, we relate ethics to Christology just as we relate salvation to Christology; we are saved in relation to Christ and we then behave our relation to Christ!

PRESUPPOSITIONS

No one of us comes neutral to our exercises of thought. We are already conditioned by influences that have shaped our lives. The first requisite of objectivity is honesty, the candid recognition of the conditioning that already affects our process of thinking. For example, one who is reacting to having been depersonalized by the dominance of authoritarian control has the processes of thought shaped by that reaction.

One of the greater secular philosophers of modern history was the German thinker, Friedrich Nietzsche. When asked why he was so negative toward the Christian faith, he responded, "I was never impressed that the members of my father's church enjoyed their religion."

Presuppositions are not to be denied or necessarily rejected; rather, they are to be recognized and objectified. Should we claim to come to an issue with no presuppositions, it would simply mean that we have not been thinking, that we have not been acting as responsible persons. The objectivity which we want to achieve is found through an honest statement of our presuppositions and a willingness to hold them in reserve while we hear other positions and examine the issues as openly as the process permits at a given time.

CONTEXTUALISM

Having traveled on most continents and in scores of countries, sharing in seminars, preaching missions, and pastors' conferences, I have a practical view of cross-cultural communication. Beyond the significant experience of working with and through many interpreters, helping them understand the meanings that I wanted to communicate so that they would put that meaning into their language and context rather than try to simply translate words by rote and thereby miss the meaning, I have come to appreciate and understand to some degree what we call in missiology *contextualization*.

We do not all think alike, but in broad strokes we think American, Chinese, Indian, Japanese, Latin, African, European, and so on. But even this obvious fact is too simple a generalization. In a given country we have different regions, cultural and racial differences, varying educational achievements, professions, religious or secular bias, and many other factors which condition our thinking. To understand one another we must communicate with awareness of the meanings that arise in context and which determine the nature of our thinking.

None of us can live without a skin and, just so, none of us can live without a culture. While culture itself may be neutral, it always tends to idolatry. It calls us to idolize the form or context in which and by which we have been conditioned. Our ability to critique, to analyze, to interpret in a culture, and then to transcend a culture is a unique part of our humanness. We do not function merely by instinct, nor are we totally determined by our culture. And yet we must recognize the contextual aspects of our thinking if we are to be able to objectify concepts and do intelligible and responsible interpretation. In so doing we make the first step toward cross-cultural communication, the ability to enter into another context and to analyze and interpret another culture in its context.

Dr. James D. Hunter, a sociologist from the University of Virginia, speaks of the evangelical church as going through a profound social change.[2] He says that we are in the midst of a "culture war" which signifies a fundamental realignment in social pluralism. By this he means that orthodox and progressive parties within faith communities find that they have more in common with other orthodox or progressive exponents from different faiths than they do with persons of a differing view within their own faith community. For example, in our cultural milieu, persons are so caught up in the spirit of the age that orthodox Jews, Muslims, and Christians have more in common because of their cultural conservatism than they do with more liberal persons in their own faith group. The question, therefore, is one of authority, of the basis on which our thinking and convictions are conditioned.

To think profoundly we need to recognize the relationship between revelation and interpretation, and between interpretation and application of truth in life. We must distinguish between symbol and reality, refusing to see symbol as more than an aid and recognizing above all the Ultimate reality to which symbol points. As a consequence we can understand reality through the use of various symbols and avoid making symbols an end in themselves; we can avoid arguments over differences between symbols, when the real issue is the manner in which they do or don't witness consistently to the reality we worship. If we are less than open to the Thou of the universe, we may be worshiping at the shrine of symbol, our most easily contrived "graven image."

THE SPIRIT OF THE MIND

The Apostle Paul calls believers to "be renewed in the spirit of your minds" (Romans 12:2). This renewal is a work of God that releases one from the dominance of sin or self-centeredness. As a depressed spirit can limit one's freedom in study and research, so a spirit of self-seeking, of status seeking, of racism, of censoriousness, of negativism, or of unbelief before the examination of the truth will alter and pervert any attempt at authentic scholarship.

When we understand the nature of human sinfulness, the perversion of the self to something less than the potential for which we have been created in the image of God, we become aware that conversion to Christ makes a difference in the learning experience. When one is converted, is liberated from self and sin's dominance, the resultant freedom liberates the mind for an excellence that is impossible when the mind is clouded by sinful selfishness. The mind is a faculty of the spirit; while the brain is a part of the physical being, the mind itself functions as the spirit of human life. We do not understand all of the dynamics of the mind, or the differences between persons in the realm of intellectual ability. Observation of human achievement shows that intellectual development is determined by more than the IQ; there are the elements of the spirit of discipline, of inquiry, of creativity, of imagination, and of conscience. When the spirit of the mind is set free to engage the meanings of the truth of God, we frequently see "average" persons outstripping the "intellectuals" in various aspects of life.

TRUTH AND IDEAS

As Christians we affirm, "All truth is God's Truth," recognizing that God as Sovereign Lord, Creator, and Sustainer of life is the Source and Master of Truth. Jesus said, "I am the Way, the Truth, and the Life" (John 14:6). When before Pilate, Jesus gave witness to having a kingdom of Truth, and Pilate, immersed in his evaluation of "truths" without understanding truth, could not comprehend such a claim of ultimate Truth.

It is important to distinguish between truths and Truth; for while many things that we hold as true may be relative, depending upon the cultural setting, Truth as ultimate meaning calls us beyond the relativity of symbols to the Reality itself. But it is at this point that we ask not simply, "What is truth?" but, "What is TRUTH?" What is True in and of itself, regardless of our evaluative judgments? In the Christian sense, Truth is Person, for Jesus said, "I am the Way, the Truth, and the Life."

When we realize, as Paul wrote to the Ephesians, that "the truth is in Jesus," we will see ideas as aids to Truth but will always reach beyond to the encounter, to a relationship of faith with God Himself. Truth is the answer to the God-dimension of life. We have been created in the image of God, and although we have defaced this image, God has acted in redeeming grace to recreate that image and in so doing to share Himself as Life with us.

RESEARCH AND DOCUMENTATION

In research we always seek primary sources, either in documentation or in scientific experimentation. In documentation we dig back until we get as close to the event as possible. The process of research always seeks to find the source on which our predecessor based his or her conclusions. To understand the Christian faith, we go back to the Christ event in order to get as near to the actual event as possible. In doing so, we have to work with the four Gospels and with the letters of the apostles, and with the over 5,000 manuscripts on which our translations of these writings are based.

If we could find something earlier than the written records that we have, we would be intellectually bound to study them. In this process, whether one accepts the Christian doctrine of Inspiration of Scripture or not, one cannot as an honest researcher do other than to affirm the authority of the documents we have for the understanding of Christ, as well as for an understanding of the Christian church, the doctrines of salvation, Christian ethics, eschatology, eternal life, and so on. Our faith in the authority of the Scripture is based on its own claims, but also on the evidence of history in its very unique transmission from the original source, often oral, to the present versions that we have. No other book has such unique and major authentication in transmission.

When we see history as a window, as a way to look in on and to test the values and meanings of life, we are enabled to do meaningful research and to document cause and effect, proven values and meanings, relationships and ideals, and more. We should be secure as thinking Christians in our quest for better understandings and dare to subject all that we believe to the most careful scrutiny. God's written Word, the Bible, can stand up to the most demanding critical study, if the scholar meets it honestly on the terms of its claims.

Further, I affirm that Jesus Christ is great enough to take our questioning and our questing on every issue that we recognize in the reflections important to having an informed faith. But in our study, we must maintain an objectivity about the questioning itself, lest we move from faith to doubt by believing the questions themselves, rather than seeing them as symbols that keep prodding us to understand Reality.

HERMENEUTICS AND CHRISTOLOGY

The science of interpretation is one of the more demanding and basic exercises of thought, in theology, in philosophy, in psychology, and in fact in every area of reflection. Hermeneutics is the exercise of interpreting in our context and thought patterns the meanings that are being conveyed by words or other symbols. This exercise, more than any other, accounts for problems of conscience, of understanding basic differences between believers and nonbelievers, and between Christian and Christian!

While hermeneutics involves understanding the language and culture, genre and style, in which something was written, it also means recognizing the theological presuppositions with which we come to interpretation.

An example of this latter may be given by quoting the words of the Apostle Paul in Romans, "He who is righteous by faith shall live" (1:17). Does Paul mean, he who is *righteous* by faith shall live, or he who is righteous *by faith* shall live, or he who is righteous by faith *shall live*? With the three different emphases I have given, we have three different theologies or systems of thought. I'm quite sure that Habakkuk, in whose prophecy the statement is first found, meant the last of the three emphases, but I'm also quite sure that Paul meant the second of the three.

Another very major question in interpreting the Bible is whether we read it as a "flat book," that is, all on one level, or whether we read it as an unfolding revelation in which God had more and more to say about Himself and His will through the Old Testament until He said it fully in Christ. I accept the latter premise, believing that the full revelation or self-disclosure of God is expressed in Jesus Christ. While the whole of Scripture is God's Word written, inspired by His Spirit, it is not of the same level of value. This may be illustrated again by the comparison of a one-dollar bill and a one-hundred-dollar bill, both valid but not both of equal value. Ecclesiastes is a part of the Word of God, but we would not say that it is at the same level as the Gospel of John.

Although our education in fourth grade was valid, once we have graduated from high school we can never go back and live at the fourth grade level. While the Old Testament is a valid Word of God in His self-disclosure, we cannot go back before the Incarnation and build our system of faith and ethics on anything other than Christ. We know that the teachings of the Old Testament on slavery, on polygamy, on the nationalism of Israel, on war and extensive capital punishment, and other matters were contextually conditioned as to what God would express at their more elementary level of understanding of His self-disclosure, and were disclosures of positions above that of the surrounding cultures. But He has not left us at that level. On the road to Emmaus Jesus "explained [unfolded] to them what was said in all the Scriptures concerning Himself" (Luke 24:27). Paul says, "In the past God overlooked such ignorance, but now He commands all people everywhere to repent" (Acts 17:30).

But with a fuller understanding of God and His will in Christ, we need to continually match our increase of comprehension with an increase in commitment. Christian growth is a "Yes, Lord! Yes, Lord!" kind of experience. When we walk in the light "as He is in the light," we will be led from one level of glory to another (2 Corinthians 3:18).

Being committed to Christ does not of itself limit the thinking process, nor does it automatically make us into scholars. We must be careful lest, in our assurance of having been brought into a relationship with Ultimate Reality, we then speak with authority in areas to which we haven't applied ourselves in careful reflection. While I believe that conversion to Christ liberates the mind to be free from self-pursuits and to become more effective in thought, I believe also that we must beware of shoddy thinking. Before we were converted we sought answers, knowingly or unknowingly, to the basic issues of ultimate reality, and may have sought such reality in many areas of knowledge. But once we are converted, thinking Christianly is more than expressing the latest secular ideas with Christian terms; it means careful and demanding thinking from a Christian worldview.[1]

If we would have a Christ-shaped conscience, we need to cultivate a deep spiritual and moral understanding, to be more conscious of the global nature of His kingdom and less parochial, more informed on the meanings of the Christian faith in the rich field of history, rather than limiting ourselves to subjective experience. We are a part of the redeemed community, a part of a living tradition, and should enjoy a sense of continuity and participation in the larger Christian discourse. In the midst of contemporary pluralism we need to think together in discerning a sense of the core meanings of the Christian faith. Rather than setting boundaries of thought, we can engage the extension of the core meanings into the frontiers of thought. Christ is Lord of all of life, and we are to find His meaning for each new frontier.

6. CONSCIENCE AND JUSTICE

In the early 1950s, I was pastor of a church in Sarasota, Florida. As an outreach from our congregation, we began a work in a community on the north edge of the city known as New Town. We constructed a building and engaged people in the new venture, and soon had a small congregation of persons, black and white, worshiping together. This was before the civil rights movement, and such a venture was not popular. One Sunday evening one of our young men was helping an elderly black gentleman home from the church service when he was arrested by a policeman, called a "nigger lover," and put in jail. By the time his pastor arrived the next morning, the young man was already in khaki pants ready for the chain gang! Both black and white were suffering injustice.

We all want to be treated justly in society. The informed conscience always protests injustice. The principle and practice of justice is the basis for an ordered society. However, discovering the way of justice in our complex society calls for honesty and careful thinking.

To think Christianly means to express faith in a credible manner. A Christian lifestyle must stand the test of intellectual validity and social relevance. To think Christianly means to be a biblical realist; that is, to understand the basic meaning and intent of Scripture, to hear and to accept its authority, without making the Bible into a "flat book" as though it contains no progress of disclosure, or using it like a dictionary of proof-texts. Such realism will inform the conscience rather than let it function on the more parochial conditioning of a given culture.

We are called to think clearly and holistically, asking God for renewed minds. For the Greeks, the mind was the center of life and direction, just as the Hebrews regarded the heart as the center of life. It seems to me that the conscience could be seen as synonymous with mind or heart, as the inner directedness of a person's life. Christian thought calls for this center conscience, mind or heart, to be transformed by the renewing of the Spirit of Christ.

Reason alone will not enable people to find God, but reason can enable us to surmount barriers to an examined faith.

Reason cannot make us wholly free from mistakes, but it can enable us to detect mistakes.

Reason cannot give absolute certainty, but it can provide a dependable point of trust.

Reason cannot provide perfect understanding, but it can develop consistency in our understanding of evidence.

Reason cannot guarantee that we won't make mistakes through subjective judgment, but it will sharpen our methods of inquiry.

Reason cannot ignore conscience and still be honest with life but it can inform conscience and enable it to be relevant to life.

Dr. Elton Trueblood has said that it is "simplistic to reject a position without a careful examination of its alternatives."[1] What I ask of my secular counterparts is an openness to look honestly at alternatives. The Christian sees belief in the trustworthiness of Jesus Christ as an ultimate act of faith. And the more we center life in the love of Christ, the more we are constrained to work for justice, the more our convictions direct us in the practice of justice.

Justice is the will of God, expressed in that mountain peak of ethical emphasis of the Old Testament prophet Micah, "He has showed you, O man, what is good. And what does the Lord require of you? To act justly and to love mercy and to walk humbly with your God" (Micah 6:8).

In the Old Testament the Hebrew root word for *justice* is also translated *righteousness*. Thus we can properly speak of justice/righteousness, the understanding of which means right-relatedness.

> Justice is the safeguard of freedom,
>   the maintenance of accountability,
>   the recognition of human dignity,
>   the equity of worth,
>   the sanctity of humanness,
>   the affirmation of divine purpose.
> Justice is the prevention of exploitation.

Human rights is a Christian responsibility. Knowing that we are all alike created in the image of God, it is our Christian responsibility to treat one another justly; that is, to seek fairness and equity for each person. We are called by God to seek public justice, to work toward a consensus that can enable cooperative action. As our global village becomes more complex, we need increased political education to prepare citizens to relate to all peoples justly. There is a very convicting quotation from Dr. Martin Niemoller, writing of his experiences in the concentration camp under Hitler:

> In Germany they came first . . . for the Jews, and I didn't speak up because I wasn't a Jew. Then they came for the trade unionists, and I didn't speak up because I wasn't a trade unionist. Then they came for the Catholics, and I didn't speak up because I was a Protestant. Then they came for me, and by that time no one was left to speak up.[2]

We need to think together as to how public justice can be pursued by public law, recognizing that the effective education of all peoples for an understanding of justice is necessary if we are to interpret and support such laws. But law itself does not produce justice, or a conscience on justice. The fruit of justice/righteousness is found more fully in the lives of persons who share the righteousness of God.

JUSTICE IS RIGHTEOUSNESS

The Old Testament is filled with references to God as a God of justice. He is God for all people alike, although this was missed by many of the more parochial Jews. His concern for the poor is inescapable evidence that He purposes that all people be treated with justice. David affirms this in his psalms of praise.

> The Lord reigns forever; He has established His throne for judgment. He will judge the world in righteousness; he will govern the peoples with justice. . . . The Lord is known by His justice" (Psalm 9:7-8, 16).
> For the word of the Lord is right and true; He is faithful in all He does. The Lord loves righteousness and justice; the earth is full of His unfailing love" (33:4-5).

Justice is used interchangeably with righteousness in biblical thought. Its first meaning is not penal, dealing with the offender, but is positive, calling for deeds of righteousness. The prophets called the people of Israel to do justice toward one another, especially to the widows and to those in need. Doing justice is behaving righteously toward others.

In the Gospel of Matthew we have a bridge from the Old Testament prophecies to the Messianic Age: "Here is my servant whom I have chosen, the one I love, in whom I delight; I will put my Spirit on Him, and He will proclaim justice to the nations" (12:18). Matthew sees Isaiah's prophecy as a clear reference to Christ; as we become His disciples, we are similarly called to practice justice. We are taught by our Lord to pray, "Thy will be done on earth as it is done in heaven."

Justice calls us to pray, to hate evil, to expose oppression, to serve others in self-giving; justice constrains us to share the

107

freedom of Christ. As a Christian, I am called by love to practice justice in relation to all other people. To assure another that he or she will be treated justly provides a basis for trust. In establishing relationships, justice is far superior to a psychology of "I'm OK, you're OK" or to an acceptance promoted by flattery. While justice can be tough and can hold us to very disciplined relationships, it is mutually rewarding and enduring in these relationships.

Our concerns for justice are concerns for human rights, for human well-being, for freedom from violation, for freedom from drug-pushers, for a welfare system that actually enables the needy rather than increases their dependency, for vouchers for higher education for inner city people to be paid to the college or university as they attend, for jobs and opportunities for the powerless that will bring stability into their financial condition, for community life that will expose and correct violence.

As I consider the issues facing us today in North America, I regard the greater social issue as the gap between the haves and the have-nots, the greater moral issue as the nuclear arms build-up as a global threat and as a priority chosen over humanitarian projects, and the greater spiritual issue as three billion people who do not know about redemption in Jesus Christ.

When the church sees itself as custodian of the message of grace, and yet lacks the conviction and the compassion to share the good news that in Christ anyone can become a child of God, this is injustice. We are often guilty of enjoying the benefits that Christ has brought into our lives, while at the same time being unconcerned about sharing them as the blessings of knowing Him. Allan Walker, Methodist evangelist from Australia, has said, "Christian knowledge and awareness is now the echo of an echo of an echo, too faint to be heard!"

JUSTICE AFFIRMS HUMAN WORTH

In a 1963 conference on kingdom membership, held at Howard University in Washington, D.C., John Perkins said that we do not need to give people dignity; we need but to recognize it!

All people are created in the image of God. The call of the Scriptures is for us to treat everyone with that dignity: men and women, one race and another, rich and poor, educated and illiterate. God treats people without respect of person, and He expects us to practice a similar justice. When Abraham was praying to God for mercy upon the people in Sodom, he expressed his ultimate hope in the words, "Will not the Judge of all the earth do right?" (Genesis 19:25)

> Justice provides freedom,
> the liberty of conscience,
> the freedom to relate to others,
> the security of common accountability.
> Justice invokes integrity,
> one can trust himself to others,
> one can appeal to conscience,
> we can seek truth together.
> Justice is love passed around,
> equality demonstrated,
> righteousness actualized,
> privilege restrained.
> Justice seeks the wholeness of all peoples.

Freedom is where love and power meet in justice/righteousness. Each of us has to steward personal power. The question is how we will use our power of personality influence, our power of education, our power of resources, our power of place. It is love that prevents power from becoming tyranny. Power is used justly when it releases the potential and enables the freedom of others by respecting the intrinsic worth of every person before God.

In 1981, I was invited to address the Oakbrook Executives Club, at the Oakbrook Sheraton in suburbaban Chicago. Arriving at O'Hare field the evening before, I overheard two men speaking about a meeting at the Sheraton, so I suggested that we share a taxi. En route to the hotel one of the men turned to me and said, "Are you here for this agricultural equipment convention tomorrow?" I replied that I was to address the Oakbrook Executives Club. The man asked me what the club was. I told him what I knew about it, and then he asked, "What is your topic?" I replied, " 'Love, Power, and Freedom.' " He immediately responded, "They don't fit!" I smiled and said, "It depends upon your definitions. If you have power and have not love, there will be no freedom for there will be tyranny. But if you have power and have love, there will be freedom for you will not violate another." The man was silent for a moment, and then responded, "Young man, if you could get that message across, you could change the world."

Christian discipleship is an ethic of freedom, of the new creature being free to cry out, "Abba, Father!" We are members of the family of God, and we are assured that in God's justice/ righteousness we will be treated justly, and that in the righteousness of Christ we will be treated with a grace of mercy that enables the greater justice.

There are no second-class citizens in God's world. Our structuring of life with status and rank easily becomes an injustice when persons are limited to a class of being "our serving public." There is a difference between my being voluntarily committed to serve others and others requiring me to serve. Jesus came "not to be ministered unto but to minister," but this was a voluntary act of His own. When Paul addressed the Corinthians, he affirmed that he was their servant; but in another passage, he made clear that they were not his master; he had one Master, the Lord in heaven. There are serving roles in society which people may well choose, but it is unjust if others in that society force them to those roles of service. Our social orders are an expression of the presence or lack of justice. Justice is not a theory, but is a practice of relationships.

JUSTICE MEANS HUMAN ACCOUNTABILITY

The call to justice is a call to work with God, to pursue His goals, to walk in His will. Amid the self-interests of human nature and its expression in society, Christians are a people separated unto God. We are accountable to one another, but above all to God. We hear His majestic words through Amos the prophet, "Let justice roll on like a river, righteousness like a never-failing stream" (5:24). By virtue of the idea of justice, humanity participates in an ordered life. Such a structure orders the relationship of persons to persons and to the natural constants of life. We were called in creation to be fruitful, and to have dominion over the created order. This dominion is over things, not over one another; and it is a responsibility placed upon us for our own generation and also for the generations to come.

> Justice is fairness,
>> giving each his due,
>> providing freedom to achieve.
> Justice recognizes inequities,
>> seeking equality of opportunity,
>> and equality of results.

In 1947, General Omar Bradley, in an Armistice Day address said, "Our humanity is trapped by moral adolescents. We have too many men of science, too few men of God. The world has achieved brilliance without wisdom, and power without conscience." We need persons of justice/righteousness.

Accountability is an affirmation of the moral character of human personality. Justice/righteousness is the standard to which we are accountable. A just society educates its citizens in the nature and necessity of justice as prerequisite to freedom among its citizens. In the community of faith, God's people will seek justice in all of their relationships with each other, and will do so in the spirit of love.

JUSTICE IS EQUAL OPPORTUNITY FOR ALL

It is not easy to look with understanding at our own culture, for we are so close that we can't see the woods for the trees. Only as we develop a psychic distance from the culture of which we are a part can we analyze it and interpret the implications of justice/righteousness for our common life.

A society that does not have different expectations for inexperienced children and experienced adults is unjust.

A society that fails to consider the limiting factors of life for orphans and handicapped persons in providing social opportunities is unjust.

A husband who interprets "headship" as his right to dominate his wife is unjust.

A parent whose possessiveness limits a child's social and spiritual development is unjust.

A parent who says, "I'll let my child decide for himself when he is ready," and who yet robs the child of adequate information and exposure to make an informed decision, is unjust.

A social structure that limits opportunities for people by discrimination of race, sex, social class, or religious preference is unjust.

A legal system which does not hold the privileged accountable in the same degree to which it requires an accounting from the underprivileged is unjust.

A tax system that does not ask the more privileged to carry a proportionately larger share of the tax load is unjust.

A nationalism that promotes our own interests at the expense of others in the global village is unjust.

In 1957, Robert Lavelle, a black real estate broker in the Hill District of Pittsburgh, had low-income clients who had been turned down again and again by lending institutions of the area. Lavelle took the reigns of a local savings company, Dwelling House Savings and Loan, and rescued it from receivership, developing it by his Christian commitment to make home loans to low-income families. In his words, "Dwelling House is a haven for Christians who replace investments in high-yield accounts with investments in God's people. When you run the business differently and people ask you why, that's when you get to tell people about Christ. That is Jesus' commission."[3]

The National Conference of Catholic Bishops published a

pastoral letter in 1986 called "Economic Justice for All" that includes six moral principles for a just economy:

• Every economic decision and institution must be judged in light of whether it protects or undermines the dignity of the human person.

• Human dignity can be realized and protected only in community.

• All people have a right to participate in the economy.

• All members of society have a special obligation to the poor and vulnerable.

• The guarantee of human rights is the minimum condition for life in community.

• Society as a whole, acting through public and private institutions, has the moral responsibility to enhance dignity and protect human rights.[4]

Justice is one of the major themes of the Bible. It reflects the character of God and calls us to be godly. We see justice in God's faithfulness, including His care for the weak, the orphans, the poor, and dispossessed. Doing justice is a responsibility of those in privilege of wealth or authority. As we relate to one another in society or in the marketplace, we must work to eliminate injustice.

JUSTICE IS CORRECTING THE PROBLEM

The command to do justice is a call to behave toward others with the right motives and right actions. When we think of justice, our thoughts often turn to civil justice which calls for punishment or retribution. But at times we seek justice in restitution, when it is possible to correct a wrong. The Bible speaks of justice most frequently in a positive manner, that of right behavior, of upholding a high moral standard for all of our relations. This includes giving everyone the right to be accepted, to be involved, to be understood, to be accountable, to shape their destiny, and to have an avenue of appeal. Justice is the groundline of a peaceful society.

Jesus gave justice a prominent place in fulfilling the expectations of God for His people. He corrected selfish thinking when He told the religious leaders that although they were very careful to pay the tithe of even the smallest vegetables of the garden, they failed to observe "the weightier matters of the law — justice, mercy, and faithfulness" (Matthew 23:23). These, He said, they "ought to have done, and not to have left the other undone."

God's concern that each person is treated justly is a dominant theme in Deuteronomy, Isaiah, Amos, Matthew (5–7), and James. Called by God into fellowship with Himself, we are at the same time called into fellowship with His people. As Christians we need a new sense of solidarity with all other humans, lest our emphasis on separation from evil separate us from other persons.

> Doing justice is the praxis of love:
>   sharing with the poor,
>   liberating the oppressed,
>   lifting the fallen,
>   encouraging the weak.
> Doing justice is practicing righteousness:
>   obeying God as commander in chief,
>   sharing a new order of relationship,
>   proclaiming the good news of grace,
>   extending the love of God.

When we think of justice primarily as giving one his due, we fail to pursue the positive side of providing persons with the freedoms for a full life, the opportunities for adequate education, employment, and life securities. Justice must take into account all of the related factors in a person's life experience. Centuries ago, Augustine distinguished between the person caught stealing for simple mischief and the poor widow stealing from the market to feed her hungry children. To pursue justice is to correct the problem; for the first, this means correcting a life view, and for the latter, correcting a life situation.

The theological undergirding of this premise, that justice is the correction of the problem, is found in Paul's statement about the Atonement, that God "did it to demonstrate His justice at the present time, so as to be just and the one who justifies those who have faith in Jesus" (Romans 3:24-26). God in mercy gave His Son as our substitute on the cross, and in doing so turns us from our rebellion and estrangement; thereby, God's justice is expressed in our being reconciled to Him and He can declare that mercy has achieved His goal!

We cannot make society a paradise; but the lack of utopia does not alter the fact that we can make a difference by pursuing justice where we are. Even raising the consciousness level of the calling and character of justice will result in a safer and stronger society. This contribution is not without cost, for some will suffer for the sake of bearing witness to the justice needed in unjust situations. This is seen in the story of Nelson Mandella, imprisoned for twenty-seven years in South Africa for his stance against the injustice of apartheid. It was seen in the life and death of Dietrich Bonhoeffer, who opposed Hitler and his tyranny, declaring, "Hitler is not Lord, Jesus is Lord," and consequently suffered death at Hitler's orders. But his faith and witness live on.

JUSTICE IS CORRECTING THE OPPRESSOR

Justice calls us to render to every person his due, a place in the ordered whole and a place which is his alone. Justice binds us in obligation to each other; at the same time, justice limits our relation to the other by delineating areas which we are not to penetrate.

All achievements of life carry with them commensurate power. Since each of us has personal power, the test of Christian love and justice is in how we use that power. When power is used to exploit others, or to gain one's own advantage at the expense of others, it is unjust. It takes an unselfish spirit to use personal power for the enrichment of others. This is the test of whether we care for the freedom and well-being of all persons in society. It is scarcely honest for us to deny the presence of power; it is rather for us to commit ourselves to unselfishness and equity in the use of whatever power we have.

Jesus unmasked the powers, exposing their character:

> the religious establishment that kept people
>   in bondage to legalism,
> the violence of political forces, both the Roman
>   and the Jewish Zealots,
> the economic self-interests that cluttered
>   the temple court for the Gentiles,
> the patriarchal structures which made women
>   second-class citizens,
> the division between the wealthy and the poor
>   which created oppression.
> Jesus still unmasks the powers, exposing them
>   in each of us!

The story Jesus shared with the disciples about a woman who kept going back to the judge in an appeal for justice, until her coming repeatedly led him to respond, concludes with the declaration that God will fulfill His commitment to justice for the oppressed, His purpose of shalom for all people. This is to say that justice is a priority for God.

One of the difficult sayings of Jesus is His answer to the man who asked Him to speak to his brother about dividing the inheritance with him. "Jesus replied, 'Man, who appointed Me a judge or an arbiter between you?' Then He said to them, 'Watch out! Be on your guard against all kinds of greed; a man's life does not consist in the abundance of his possessions' " (Luke 12:14-15). The point would appear to be that Jesus wanted the man to go to his brother in the right spirit and speak for himself. This is pursuing justice.

The Christian will pursue arbitration rather than litigation. To address one another in openness and love is the first step toward arbitration. Baris has said, "Litigation is like a machine— you go in one end a pig and come out the other a sausage."

That is, we go in greedy and come out ruined. The Christian Legal Society is one voice for the settlement of issues out of court by careful arbitration.

The Mennonite Church has a conciliation ministry to enable persons with differences to enter into arbitration rather than litigation. This is built on the teachings of Jesus that call us to go first to the one with whom we have a difference; then, if the case is not answered, we take another with us so that a third person being present can more assuredly provide fairness; and then, if the case is not resolved, we involve the congregation. As a pastor, I have participated in several arbitrations. The procedure has been for both of the parties to name one or two persons; then the several persons named get together and choose others to work with them. This group, as a committee of arbitration, hears and examines the issue and agrees on the resolution. The procedure works when the initial parties have committed themselves to live with the decision of the arbitration group.

Justice is a community concern. We seek together to secure justice for each. In doing so we also secure justice for the whole. This is a major contribution that the Christian community can make to the social order. While we are citizens with one another in society, we are first of all citizens of the kingdom of heaven!

JUSTICE IS CARING COMMUNITY

While it may be, as Emil Brunner has said, that love is justice passed around, it may also be said conversely that justice is love passed around! The sense of responsibility engendered by the Christian faith is to give others their "right," that which belongs to them.

As members of the body of Christ we care for one another, we respect one another, and we secure the freedom and right of all for self-fulfillment in and with the group. This is the order of life which we learn from the Master.

Justice is Christological:
  it is interpreted in Christ,
  it is empowered by Christ in love,
  it is shared under the rule of Christ.
Justice is a principle of Christ's kingdom:
  He is the sovereign Ruler,
  He sets the agenda,
  He provides the norms.

The Prophet Hosea speaks for God in expressing His covenant of mercy, love, and compassion in a context of justice: "I will betroth you to Me forever; I will betroth you in righteousness and justice, in love and compassion. I will betroth you in faithfulness, and you will acknowledge the Lord" (Hosea 2:19-20). God has called us into a relationship of grace, a salvation which Paul says is not of works of righteousness which we have done but by God's grace, not by works, so that no one can boast. "For we are God's workmanship created in Christ Jesus to do good works, which God prepared in advance for us to do" (Ephesians 2:10). From the Prophet Hosea, we discover that these works which God has previously ordained are the works of justice/righteousness.

A major problem in western society is the extent to which our individualism has isolated us from one another. The average American finds it almost impossible to share intimately with another. Intimacy involves trust, familiarity, closeness, and understanding. Intimacy means involvement with another person, a willingness to be vulnerable, an interest in sharing pain and defeat as well as successes. There is no full justice apart from a depth of compassion that brings to another a sense of self-worth. Justice enables others to find their greater fulfillment; it is not a "handout" as much as a "handup."

Injustice is the expression of our self-interest that negates the freedoms of others. Racism, in its many forms, is one of the more blatant forms of social injustice. It is when we cross cultural lines to truly learn to know our neighbors, sense their problems and needs, enter into their loves and pleasures, participate

118

in the common issues of life, that our attitudes change. As the words of the Old Testament express it, "We are bound together in the bundle of life" (1 Samuel 25:29).

As thinking Christians we must discover how to apply biblical principles to the orders of the common life. This means more than quoting the Bible in support of some position. We need to think Christianly, in depth, as a community of believers. In business this involves management, marketing, accounting, advertising, insurance, information systems, banking, real estate, investments, production, public relations, and organizational behavior.

To apply Christian principles to public policy we consider income distribution, unemployment, health care, national resources, education, welfare, monetary systems, government regulations, national security, foreign trade, agriculture, and taxation.

A major problem in our society is our implicit worship of materialism. We try to serve two masters, God and mammon, and in doing so we lose God! The church of North America has compromised the Gospel through this materialism. We seem to be more concerned for size and status than for sanctity and service.

Several years ago a Russian Baptist delegation was visiting churches in the United States. They were shown through a large church in Texas, and were told that the annual budget was over $7 million. They expressed appropriate amazement over a church having a budget of that size. The next week they visited a large horse ranch and were told that a fine stud from the stables had just sold for $7 million. One of the pastors commented, "Oh, then that was just a one-horse church that we visited!"

We must beware of letting the status quo mentality of our society, the satisfaction with achievements that can be measured by material factors, dominate in our lives. We are called to share the values of Jesus as we share the kingdom of Jesus. As Paul wrote to the Romans, we should not let the world squeeze us into its mold (12:2). While we as Christians are separated unto

God and His kingdom, we are fellow citizens in society. While the patterns of our behavior are not set by the world, we do not surrender the world to evil. We are called to be "salt to the earth" and "light to the world," to both enrich and preserve. The redeemed community does not walk in darkness but shares the Light of Life.

JUSTICE IS FREEDOM FROM TYRANNY

To deal justly with others means to seek their freedom and fulfillment. To attempt to control others is to subject their personality potential to yours. An understanding of loving your neighbor as yourself includes your responsibility to seek the same freedom for fulfillment in the other person's life as you seek for your own.

The human conscience cries out against injustice, against tyranny and the violation of a person's life. This calls for honest confrontations of such problems as child abuse, spouse abuse, racism, violence, and all forms of unfairness to others. Justice means that we seek not only the well-being but the fulfillment of the potential of the life of each person with whom we relate. This is not a matter measured only by sins of commission but by sins of omission.

Through the years of our marriage, Esther and I have supported each other. When I was going to graduate school she supported me; and later, when our children were at an age and stage in school where she felt free to pursue graduate studies in art, I supported her. In the years following we have worked together in education and in pastoral ministry as a team, a relation in which I enjoy seeing her achieve meaningfully in her commissionings in sculpture and in lecture assignments. In turn we have found the way to share our different roles in a manner that respects each other's freedom in our respective areas.

The matter of justice and injustice is often read more easily when seen in the larger social issues of life. But the principle of justice should be present in every interpersonal relation. In disciplining children, we should beware of punishing a misdemeanor when we are emotionally distraught. In a matter such as family budgeting, we should work together in achieving fairness to each partner and avoiding undue pressure on either. In social relations, we should express not only tolerance of persons with differing views but fairness to them in exercising their choices.

I find it a searching study to interface the Beatitudes of Matthew 5 with the contrasting Woes of Matthew 23. Jesus is speaking in both passages, offering blessing for those who are open to God and woe to those who would misuse God.

"BLESSED are the poor in spirit, for theirs is the kingdom of heaven" (Matthew 5:3).	"WOE to you, teachers of the law and Pharisees, you hypocrites! You shut the kingdom of heaven in men's faces" (Matthew 23:13).
"BLESSED are those who mourn, for they will be comforted" (5:4).	"WOE to you, teachers of the law and Pharisees, you hypocrites! You . . . win a single convert . . . you make him twice as much a son of hell as you are" (23:15).
"BLESSED are the meek, for they will inherit the earth" (5:5).	"WOE to you, blind guides! You say . . . if anyone swears by the gold of the temple, he is bound by his oath" (23:16).
"BLESSED are those who hunger and thirst for righteousness, for they will be filled" (5:6).	"WOE to you, teachers of the law and Pharisees, you hypocrites! You give a tenth of your spices — mint, dill, and cummin. But you have neglected the more important matters of the law — justice, mercy, faithfulness" (23:23).

"BLESSED are the merciful, for they will be shown mercy" (5:7).

"WOE to you, teachers of the law and Pharisees, you hypocrites! You clean the outside of the cup and dish, but inside they are full of greed and self-indulgence" (23:25).

"BLESSED are the pure in heart, for they will see God" (5:8).

"WOE to you, teachers of the law and Pharisees, you hypocrites! You are like whitewashed tombs, which look beautiful on the outside but on the inside are full of dead men's bones" (23:27).

"BLESSED are the peacemakers, for they will be called the sons of God" (5:9).

"WOE to you, teachers of the law, and Pharisees, you hypocrites! . . . You say, 'If we had lived in the days of our forefathers, we would not have taken part with them in shedding the blood of the prophets.' So you testify against yourselves that you are the descendants of those who murdered the prophets"(23:29-30).

"BLESSED are those who are persecuted because of righteousness, for theirs is the kingdom of heaven" (5:10).

"I am sending you prophets and wise men and teachers. Some of them you will kill and crucify; others you will flog in your synagogues" (23:33).

Jesus' confrontation of the religious leaders offers unusual insights into His personality. In these verses from Matthew, He pronounces judgment upon religious leaders for their lack of compassion, their inconsistencies, and their failure to seek justice for all. Israel had lost its universal vision, had turned God into a national deity to serve their own cause.

Jesus' act of cleansing the temple is to be seen in the same manner as the confrontation in Matthew 23. When Jesus came into the temple court and found it cluttered with the merchants who actually robbed the people by refusing any but the proper Jewish coins and charging exorbitant exchange, or by selling only those animals for sacrifices that the priests personally approved, this was enough to arouse His anger. But in addition, they were in the court of the Gentiles, and had so cluttered it with the Jewish business that the Gentiles could not get in to worship.

Jesus made a rope whip and drove from the temple court "both the sheep and the oxen," and overturned the money changers' tables, ordering them to take their wares out as this was to be a house of prayer "for all peoples." There is no evidence that He laid a whip on any person. He spoke to them in forthright and forceful directives and overturned their tables, but He evidently used the whip on the sheep and the oxen. To use this passage to justify the use of violence is to miss its primary intent and to fail to see the concern for justice that motivated the Master. In contrast to the religious leaders of Israel, "Jesus went through all the towns and villages, teaching in their synagogues, preaching the good news of the kingdom and healing every disease and sickness. When He saw the crowds, He had compassion on them, because they were harassed and helpless, like sheep without a shepherd" (Matthew 9:35-37).

In this awareness the Lausanne Covenant says, "All of us are shocked by the poverty of millions and disturbed by the injustices which cause it. Those of us who live in affluent circumstances accept our duty to develop a simple lifestyle in order to contribute more generously to both relief and evangelism."[5]

Many evangelical Christians are very reluctant to accept the fact that poverty for the millions is directly linked to injustice, to power struggles that increase the gap between the "haves" and the "have-nots." We need to hear the Master say to us, "I was hungry and you gave Me something to eat, I was thirsty and you gave Me something to drink, I was a stranger and you invited Me in, I needed clothes and you clothed Me, I was sick and you looked after Me, I was in prison and you came to visit Me. . . . Whatever you did for one of the least of these brothers of Mine, you did for Me" (Matthew 25:35-40). It is difficult for me not only to be present among the poor, as I have been in a measure for the past nine years as an inner city pastor in Washington, D.C., but to form an alignment with them that can impact the secular structures for their good.

John V. Taylor, reviewing David Livingstone's correspondence, gives us a very searching insight.

Shortly after Livingstone's home station and most of his possessions had been destroyed by Boer commandos as a reprisal for his support of the Bakwena people, he wrote in a letter to the London Missionary Society: "Everywhere there is a strong feeling of independence springing up. The English, as a nation, have lost character and honour. The destruction of my property is a fortunate thing for me. There is not a native in the country but knows now for certain on whose side I am."[6]

Such identification can be equally costly today for those who would stand for justice. Soon after returning from our stint of service in India, Esther and I went to see the movie *Cry Freedom*. We were deeply moved by the price one family had to pay for seeking justice for blacks caught in the grip of apartheid. When we call the roll of some forty wars currently in our world, of the injustices in the caste system of India with nearly a billion people, of the racism in South Africa and many other countries including some attitudes in America, of the genocide in Cambodia, of the violence between the Israelis and the Palestinians, of the oppression and violence in Central and South America, we should be aware that God is saying, "The voice of thy brother's blood cries out to Me from the ground" (Genesis 4:10).

The call to Christian mission must be heard as a call to a mission of social justice as well as to spiritual fellowship. God's salvation is a restoration for the whole of life. For Christian missions to emphasize the importance of physical healing, while at the same time not being equally concerned for social and emotional healing, is hardly consistent. For missions to "reach down" to the poor and offer them a salvation that promises life eternally, but fail to share the eternal quality of life in God's will now is not a full gospel. To go out in mission under the security of our country in its commitment to stand by its citizens for justice, and at the same time to fail to seek the same social justice for those among whom we minister, is to lack genuine compassion.

In the spirit of Christ we are called to pursue justice for the oppressed, to seek freedom for those who are in bondage, and to announce the time of the Lord's favor. The kingdom of God is among us, for the King is with us. We are heralds of the new word of grace, of the new quality of life, of the new community of the Spirit. Now there is neither Greek nor Jew, for He is our peace; He has broken down the barrier and brought to birth a new humanity, so making peace (Ephesians 2:14-18).

JUSTICE IS MISSION

God loves the world. Christ died for the people of the world. Being exalted at the right hand of God, Christ is now Lord of all, interested in each person coming into the grace of God. Of the coming mission of the Messiah, the Prophet Isaiah said, "In faithfulness He will bring forth justice; He will not falter or be discouraged till He establishes justice on earth" (42:3-4).

As Jesus' disciples, His ministers of reconciliation, we are involved in a mission of justice in providing equal opportunity for all to come into God's family. But this means that we must understand people and meet them where they are. A schoolteacher cannot make the same demands on the slower students as on the advanced, for to do so would be unjust. Just so, justice does not expect the same of all people.

Aristotle inquired into the nature of justice, recognizing the close connection of justice with equality and seeing a dual nature in justice. First, he spoke of simple contractual justice which gives the same to each person. Second, he spoke of proportional or distributive justice, giving the same to each according to a scale of inequality.

Jesus called for justice not according to difference in persons but difference in opportunity. In Jesus' Parable of the Talents, in which one received five talents, another two, and another one, justice is evidenced in that the Lord expected proportionate results conditioned by the opportunity.

In the Book of Proverbs there is a unique passage in which wisdom speaks in the first person. This passage is thought by scholars to correspond to the use of *logos* in John 1. In Proverbs 8, wisdom speaks of being the source of justice by which princes rule, and of leading in the way of righteousness. This is a beautiful passage on the richness of life for a person who walks with wisdom and with shalom as their portion of grace, because wisdom is an extension of God Himself into our lives (Proverbs 8:12-36). This prophetic vision of the Incarnation identifies Wisdom as being in the presence of God from eternity, extending divine love and justice to us.

> A Christian vision sees life whole,
>   not separating the sacred from the social,
>   not classifying people according to merit,
>   not accepting prejudice or inequality.
> A Christian vision seeks God's will for all,
>   endeavoring to sanctify relationships,
>   lifting life above physical instincts,
>   glorifying God in human relations.

It is our mission as Christians to both pray "Thy will be done on earth as it is in heaven" and to work for such righteousness and justice in life. As agents of reconciliation we are God's ambassadors in society, representing our Sovereign, giving witness to the higher will of God, calling people to live by the highest ethics of humanness. As Christians we are the salt of the earth, enriching, preserving, purifying, contributing to all around us. We are the light of the world, bringing direction and under-standing to the thoughts and choices that people are called to share.

Justice is love spread around. Love is not passive but active, and as such it seeks justice for all. We love our children too much not to give them a good example of faith. We love the church too much not to work for its continuing renewal and relevance. We love our country too much to allow voices and influences to move us down the road of violence and war. We should love our global village enough to promote the kingdom of God and its values worldwide! We do this through the many Christian disciples who carry this expression of love and justice outside of the four walls of the churches into the orders of common life. The words of George Macleod express this most effectively:

> I simply argue that the cross be raised again at the center of the marketplace as well as on the steeple of the church. I am recovering the claim that Jesus was not crucified in a cathedral between two candles, but on a cross between two thieves; on the town garbage heap, at a crossroads so cos-mopolitan that they had to write His name in Hebrew and in Latin and in Greek, at the kind of place where cynics talk smut and thieves curse, and soldiers gamble. Because that is where He died. And that is what He died about. And that is where churchmen should be and what church-men should be about.[7]

JUSTICE AND THE USE OF PRIVILEGE AND POWER

Emil Brunner said, "The essence of the State is not justice but power."[8] That is to say, the state is the unified will binding on each individual. This is the power of the political order. Throughout history there has been an affinity between anarchy and injustice, and between sovereign power and justice. The justice of a political system is a major factor in its stability, and this justice is dependent upon just law.

In a state of anarchy, there is no more justice than in a totalitarian state. Unless there is law, the most upright person cannot live in peace if his neighbor does not respect his rights. As Christians we must witness to the state, calling it to live up to the highest level of its claims for law and justice. And perhaps the phrase "law and justice" should have priority over "law and order"!

Not only do we witness to persons in power who are sympathetic to the Christian values we espouse, but we also witness to persons in structures where they make no Christian claim:

• To call persons within the structure to become Christ's disciples.

• To call those responsible to hold the structure accountable to its own goals and ideals.

• To challenge sub-Christian patterns to values and goals that are higher.

• To dare to exercise and clarify the grounds for conscientious refusal to participate, when the role is not compatible with Christian discipleship.

We should appeal to the ideals of the American political community, doing so as genuine Christians but on the grounds of values shared by the wider political community. As Christians we do not attempt to take over the political structures to use their power, but we seek to live by the greater spiritual power of faith.

Faith survives the power of political forces. While the power of Caesar that executed Christ has risen and fallen, as have similar powers through the centuries, the cross of Christ continues its transforming work in the world. The cross is to be raised in the marketplace, in the factory, in the office, and not only on the steeples of church buildings. It is to be laid upon the heart of the disciple and not simply worn on a gold chain as an ornament. The cross is the symbol of a death that is overcome by love. And this love can give birth to a new life of justice.

When the Christian Church recovers the conviction of an

identification with the risen Christ that results in newness of righteousness/justice in action, the church will be relevant in society. But unless we see salvation as a present relationship that changes things for us both vertically and horizontally, we will fail to participate in the full meaning of redemption. As evangelical Christians, we need to balance our emphasis on the "fallenness" of humanity with an emphasis on the "redeemed community." We are a new people in Christ.

Dr. Lesslie Newbigin tells the moving story of the Russian Communist leader, Bukharin, speaking at an anti-God rally at Kiev in the 1920s. Following Bukharin's presentation, a priest from the Russian Orthodox Church asked to say a word to the crowd. Facing the people, he lifted his hand and shouted the ancient liturgical Easter greeting, "The Lord is risen!" With one great voice, like the sound of the crash of mighty waves against a rocky cliff, the people responded joyfully, "He is risen indeed!" Bukharin had their answer, the answer of faith, of confidence in the lordship of the risen Savior.

7. CONSCIENCE AND PEACE

In the fall of 1983, there were two letters written to President Reagan by Lukas Haas, the little lad who was a lead actor in the film *Testament*. The letters speak for themselves.

October 30, 1983
Dear President Reagan Sir,
I hope that you will stop the bomb. Because I don't want to die, my friends don't want to die, and plus you're an elderly gentleman so you won't be on the earth much longer, but we are going to. You don't know how we feel about the bombs. Just imagine how it would feel if you were a kid and had to worry about nuclear war. Don't you love a little child that you know who you can talk to about bombs? I bet if you could see things like him you wouldn't be doing the bombs right now cause you know how it feels. Does your wife Nancy think bombs are good too? Because I saw her on the drugs program and she doesn't want kids to die from drugs so why should she want them to die from bombs? Thank you and good-bye.

U.S. Citizen,
Lukas Haas, Age 7½

P.S. I am in a movie that's in the theaters now and it's called *Testament*. It is about a nuclear bomb and may you please watch it. Good-bye, Lukas.

November 12, 1983
Dear Reagan Sir,
I still don't like the bombs because you think they won't do anything bad to us. Because you just think they'll hurt the other country. But it will hurt the whole world, maybe even the moon and some stars. My name is Lukas. May you please stop the bombs. I've told you this before and I meant what I said. You didn't answer my letter yet. Did you get it? I'm the child who was in *Testament*, a movie about bombs so you will not make bombs.

May you please see the movie? It's called *Testament* and I bet it's in your hometown. I know you were an actor and you might've been in this movie if you were a child and had to worry about bombs, President Reagan! I think you shouldn't be so scared of the Russians. And you should send some reporters down and say, "Russians! Don't be afraid of us . . . we won't hurt you and may you please not hurt us!" Humans need to talk to each other. There's a bully in my class named Marco who says mean things to me and does mean things to me. That's just like the Russians are doing to us and we're doing to them. You've got to speak to them!

Dear Mr. President, I promise to talk to Marco if you will talk to the President of Russia.

Your fellow citizen,
Lukas Haas, Age 7½[1]

President Reagan did talk with the Russians, and we've kept on talking, and what a remarkable moment in history! The changes that began to happen in the end of 1989 have been almost unbelievable. And much of it has followed the example of Lech Walesa of Poland, whose nonviolent expressions led to an admission of the emptiness of the communist system and the need for a more democratic approach to life. In this political change, the violence of Romania stood out in stark contrast.

It is strange that the evangelical church has so little conscience on peacemaking and such strong convictions in support of military strength. In many settings one almost needs to apologize to an audience before speaking of peace. During a recent address, I identified myself as a Christian pacifist. After my speech a woman angrily confronted the president of the college about my using their platform for "political reasons." His response was proper, that for me pacifism was not political but theological, and a question of lifestyle. This issue, as much as any, divides the church and exposes the differences in the ways our consciences have been informed or programmed.

Jesus said, "Blessed are the peacemakers, for they shall be called sons of God" (Matthew 5:9). In announcing the Messiah's coming birth, Isaiah called Jesus "the Prince of Peace" (Isaiah 9:6). Centuries later, the Apostle Paul said of Him, "He Himself is our peace" (Ephesians 2:14). Jesus said of Himself, "For I did not come to judge the world, but to save it" (John 12:47). His life of love and his death in love both taught and modeled the way of nonviolence in His confrontation with evil. Jesus taught us by word and deed to love our enemies, to turn the other cheek as a strategy of operation, and to bear the cross as an instrument of change.

Why is it that we have so little conscience against violence and war? One of the most effective modern proponents of nonviolence was Martin Luther King Jr. He wrote to his opponents:

> We shall match your capacity to inflict suffering by our capacity to endure suffering. We shall meet your physical force with soul force. Do to us what you will, and we shall continue to love you . . . Be assured that we will wear you down by our capacity to suffer. One day we shall win freedom, but not only for ourselves. We shall so appeal to your heart and conscience that we shall win you in the process, and our victory will be a double victory.[2]

As a disciple of Jesus Christ, I cannot take the life of another for whom Christ died, for I want that person to become my brother or sister in Christ. Furthermore, as a disciple I must follow the example of my Master! Jesus stood before the State and made decisions as to how to deal with evil, decisions that are expressions of the Word of God in Christ. Moreover, Jesus taught that we are to love our neighbors as ourselves, and in this He included our enemies. While we were yet sinners, yet His enemies, Christ died for us. As His disciples we are to live in His pattern of love.

This concept of discipleship is basic to our understanding of the character of the "new man." Being born again, born from above, means being born into a new relationship, into the kingdom of God (John 3:3, 5). The priority for the church is to call a people into the will of God; it is not to create a new structure in society, but to enrich society through this new people.

When we see the church as God's priority in the world, then we will see the state as providing a framework in which the church can be the church. While God's will is one, He recognizes that humanity will have one of two responses, a response of faith or a response of self-defense.

A member of our congregation was U.S. Consul General with the Embassy in Managua, Nicaragua. In one letter, he related some of the difficulties he faced: "The peace position you have taught us at the church looks awfully good from down here; however, sometimes one is tempted to use violence to meet some problems; but one thing I've learned, you can't be a little bit violent!" That last statement is of major importance, "you can't be a little bit violent." The statement is consistent with Jesus' emphasis that violence begets violence.

The separation of the church from the state is not simply a structural separation, but a separation of faith and ethics, of commitment and compassion. A Christian level of ethics is not expected from society in general. Peacemaking is not a matter of the church trying to run the state; rather, it is a matter of Christian citizens being a right influence on the state. As George Failing has said, "If the ordering of the state becomes the business of the church, the ordering of the church will become the business of the state."³

Much of our position depends upon how we understand the Bible. Our differences of conviction arise from the ways in which Christians read the Bible. What we believe is not necessarily what the Bible says, but what we understand it to say! Once we admit this, we can talk with one another, pray with one another, and seek together to test what others understand the biblical message to be.

We are not like the Swede who said he was not going to get his car waxed because the Bible says, "In the last days men will wax worse and worse!" We must read the Bible in context, understand its basic intent, and apply it honestly in the context in which we live.

PEACE IS RENUNCIATION OF HOSTILITY

Peace is one of the sweetest words in our language: peace with God, peace in one's life, peace at home, peace with one's neighbor, peace between peoples, peace between nations! It is a positive word, a dynamic word, but at the same time a meek word. As Christians, we are a people of peace; governments are to keep the peace; police officers are referred to as "peace officers"; the United Nations has "peace forces"; we seek to live at peace, and we pray for peace.

Even so, there is so much violence in the world. We see it from city streets to battlefields, from family problems to class struggles, from social structures to racial antagonism. We, therefore, who follow the Prince of Peace are called to become peacemakers; and as such, we shall be known as the children of God (Matthew 5:9). And yet, many Christians are very hesitant to speak out for peace or to work to achieve it.

It is evident in this issue that we have bought into the world's materialistic philosophy of believing that we must guard what we have, even with the use of violence. Some Christians seem to believe that the security of their possessions is more important than human life. True, we should value the material order that God has created and given to us, but we should place higher value on people created in God's image. From the Christian perspective, every person, across cultural and racial lines, is seen as our fellow, created in the image of God.

Peacemaking maximizes what we have in common and minimizes our differences.

Peacemaking emphasizes forgiveness and rejects revenge, seeking the well-being of the other person.

Peacemaking looks beyond the issue to the person, seeking ways to resolve the problem by arbitration.

Peacemaking means confronting in love, talking with one rather than about one.

Peacemaking involves a willingness to suffer loss, including loss of face, for the joy of helping another to "save face."

When we repent, we renounce the way of life characterized by rebellion against God. In this renunciation we say no to selfishness and to the misuse of others. This misuse includes vice, sensuality, injustice, and violence. If we are to know peace, we must begin by the positive actions of love, compassion, justice, and nonresistant love. Peace is the consequence of godliness; it is not the result of works of the flesh but is a fruit of the Spirit.

> Peace is harmony
> > between God and people,
> > between people and people,
> > between people and nature.
> Peace is a vision of life;
> > it is a process,
> > it is a method of arbitration,
> > it is overcoming in conflict.

Hostility is a defense mechanism that enslaves life rather than frees it. Enmity leads in some measure to being formed by the opponent, by virtue of the attention given to the adversary. Someone has said that our enemies are closer to us than our friends, because they are on our minds more. To be hostile is to create a barrier, to insulate ourselves from others, but it is also to strike out, to defend our space rather than to share it. As a consequence, society is the loser, for life is enriched by sharing with others rather than by excluding them. Reconciliation involves confrontation, but with acceptance, not with hostility.

Reconciliation is costly—it cost our Lord the cross. It means loving not just peace and justice, but people. It means that we hate injustice and violence, not people. Once we separate the issue from the person, we can move to a renewal of relationship. We should not regard peace as simply the absence of physical violence but as a sharing of love and justice. Reconciliation usually means overcoming ourselves rather than overcoming our adversaries, for only then can we relate with courage, generosity, and forgiving love.

PEACE IS RECOGNITION OF PERSON-WORTH

In 1945 Dr. Robert Oppenheimer led a group of scientists in developing and testing the first atomic bomb. On a day known as Trinity, the bomb was exploded, and three weeks later it was dropped on Hiroshima, with the second one being dropped five days later on Nagasaki. This was done even though on the day after Trinity, Dr. Oppenheimer had said the bomb should be put away and never used.

When the bomb was dropped over Hiroshima, 100,000 people died in nine seconds! Rather than hear the words of Oppenheimer, his successor, Teller, pushed for bigger bombs, and the hydrogen bomb was developed by 1954. We now have bombs 4,000 times stronger than the one dropped on Hiroshima!

Jacques Ellul has written, "Violence is always a process, which once begun cannot be stopped. Violence only begets more violence, unless mercy and forgiveness intervene."[4] This is another way of expressing the meaning of Jesus' words, "They that take the sword will perish by the sword." In contrast, God calls us to live in love, to create a community of fellowship that is transcultural, transracial, and transnational. To do this we need to develop a network of Christians around the world.

As Christians transcend the lines of division created between peoples, we can create friendship and associations of goodwill across national lines; we can develop associations that governments by their nature are incapable of creating.[5] As Christians we have a unique opportunity, for we are a part of a global family of faith. If the church fails at its mission of being peacemakers, we will have failed God and our world, for there is no other body with the potential for the same transnational fellowship. This should be recognized as a vital part of the philosophy of missions for the evangelical church.

> Peace is love in action; it is
>   authentic compassion,
>   actualized friendship,
>   acceptance with differences.
> Peace is love — acting.

> Peace is the refusal to be tyrannized; it is
>   freedom under oppression,
>   freedom to suffer without retaliation,
>   freedom to continue loving.
> Peace is liberation of spirit.

> Peace is promoting another's well-being; it is
>   enabling another to trust,
>   enhancing another's security,
>   engaging another in reconciliation.
> Peace is enjoying "common grace" together.

Peace is the expression of our valuing of persons. The expression, "Life is cheap," used by Americans as descriptive of Vietnamese culture, demonstrated a failure of understanding. Life is important in every culture. The tragedy is if Americans imposed this expression as a judgment on another culture to diminish our own sense of guilt in violating the life-rights of other peoples.

137

There is no noble way to take the life of another human; there is no just way to kill. Even if we face a moral dilemma, the inescapable death would still be a tragedy of injustice against life.

In the fourth century, there lived an Italian monk named Tellemacus. He had a sense that the Lord was telling him to go to Rome, and so he packed his meager bag and made the long trek to the city. As he entered the streets he heard loud shouts and saw crowds of people moving toward the amphitheater. He followed the crowd, and climbed to the top tier to find a seat. As he looked down into the arena he saw two gladiators begin to fight each other. As he watched, horrified, he suddenly leaped to his feet and started shouting, "In the name of Christ, stop!" The crowd around him called out for him to be quiet, but he shouted all the more. He began to make his way down through the bleachers, shouting, "In the name of Christ, stop!" When he got to the bottom he jumped into the arena shouting, and one of the gladiators flipped his sword at him and pierced his body. As the monk lay gasping out his life, he was still saying, "In the name of Christ, stop."

The arena grew silent as the two gladiators stood looking down at the body of the little monk, his words in their minds. Suddenly one of them turned and hurled his sword across the arena. The other watched, then hurled his sword after the first, and then the two walked out of the arena. Then the people got up and began filing out of the stands until the arena was empty. That was the last time gladiators fought in the arena in Rome, all because a monk had the conviction to shout, "In the name of Christ, stop!"

PEACE IS RECONCILIATION, NOT NEGATIVISM

One of the most marvelous Christological passages on peace is Ephesians 2:14-18, where Paul speaks of Christ as our peace. He relates peace to the atonement and grounds the ethic of peace in the redemptive work of Christ. Here we are introduced to the greatest conceivable social change—Jew and Gentile becoming one new humanity. This social change is inauguarated through and by the cross. The redemptive and the ethical are united by a high Christology, for we should relate our behavior to Christ in the same way that we relate our beliefs to Christ.

It is unfortunate that many Christians do not take seriously enough God's acts of grace in creating one new humanity between Jew and Gentile. Attitudes toward the Israeli and Palestinian conflict express not a Christological but an Old Testament perception that endorses Israel's conduct in spite of the injustice, violence, and dispossession perpetrated upon their Palestinian neighbors. God loves both equally, Christ died for both alike, and the removal of the barrier by the cross calls people from each group to become one new humanity. This is an extension of the peace of God into the social aspects of life. Peace is not only a vertical reality between us and God, but also a horizontal reality extended from and by the people of God.

God's kingdom has the character of shalom:
the fullness of life in God's covenant,
the fullness of human well-being.
God's kingdom is rooted in His acts:
liberating a people from bondage,
freeing a people for righteousness.

When God called Gideon to be the deliverer for Israel, the first significant act Gideon performed was to build an altar. He named it Jehovah Shalom, "the God who brings wholeness, who brings peace." The good news to the powerless, to the dispossessed, is that God cares for all people alike, that He identifies with each of us where we are, to bring us to shalom. What a difference it would make if each white person looked at each black person as equally made in God's image for Shalom, if each Jewish person looked at each Arab person as equally made in God's image for Shalom. He Himself is our peace and He makes the two to become one new humanity!

As a disciple of Christ I must call the Jewish community to

139

love and neighborliness to the Palestinian, to nonviolence and acceptance, and to the fulfillment of Isaiah 19, where God calls for united semetic peoples. God says, "In that day Israel will be the third, along with Egypt and Assyria, a blessing on the earth. The Lord Almighty will bless them saying, 'Blessed be Egypt my people, Assyria my handiwork, and Israel my inheritance' " (19:24-25).

To the Palestinians I must as a disciple of Christ call for love and nonviolence, for forgiveness and acceptance. I believe that if the Palestinians would sit in on the West Bank and Gaza until they fill all of the jails of Israel, they would do more to arouse the moral conscience of the world to the inequity in the Middle East than they will by the use of violence.

One of our most difficult problems is how the church can work for peace when its own people are so divided by nationality, culture, race, denominationalism, theological views and ideological positions. We must pray for and seek the ability to hear each other, to distinguish the necessary from the desirable. We need to work together for the enrichment of the world community and for the securing of justice and a resultant measure of peace in the global village. With the recent report that the world population is growing by 200,000 each day, some predict that by the turn of the century the earth will not be able to support the population. Working for peace becomes an immediate and absolute necessity. Only by sharing will we be able to live together.

PEACE IS A POSITIVE, FORGIVING GRACE

The peace to which we have been called is an essential aspect of the new community of disciples. If it is to be the reality, we must permit the peace of Christ to rule in our hearts — literally, to be the umpire and call the strikes.

The writer of Hebrews tells us, "Follow peace with all men and holiness, without which [following] no one shall see the Lord" (12:14). Because *follow* is in the imperative, the issue here is not the degree of holiness we have attained, but whether we are following holiness and walking with Jesus. If this interpretation is correct, it would then mean that following peace and following holiness are to be held together, so that without the following of peace and of holiness, we will not see the Lord.

Since Jehovah is a God of peace, since Jesus is the Prince of Peace, and since the fruit of the Spirit is "love, joy, peace . . . " there is no question about whether one who is a child of God is to live by His peace. The one born of God will express the character of the Father. Thus Jesus said, "Be merciful, just as your Father is merciful" (Luke 6:36).

> The peacemaker
>   works in love,
>   seeking justice;
> The compassionate
>   hear the cry of the oppressed,
>   identify with the righteous cause.

When we understand that we are members of one body, we may then be able to understand that we are called to peace. God is creating a people reconciled to Himself and to each other. There is only one command for us: love. We are to love God and to love humanity. As D.L. Moody said, "A great many people are trying to make peace, but that has already been done. God has not left it for us to do; all we have to do is to enter into it."[6] And while Mr. Moody served as a chaplain to soldiers, he said, "When it comes to the question of war, I am a Quaker."

Peace is the extension of love to others. It is accepting them, affirming them, valuing them, freeing them. To work for peace means that we forgive others their offenses, we take our thumb off, we release them into freedom. Persons need to be released from being controlled, physically and emotionally. As we share compassionate understanding we build peace.

Alan Paton's *Ah, But Your Land Is Beautiful* gives a moving portrayal of South Africa. Judge Oliver accepted the invitation of a black pastor to take part in the Holy Thursday foot-washing service at The Holy Church of Zion. The judge washed the feet of a black woman, following Jesus' example, and kissed them. Tears filled the eyes of the congregation. The press gave the happening publicity and Mr. Oliver was denied a chief judgeship in Apartheidsville. When the black pastor called to apologize, Judge Oliver said, "Taking part in your service on Maundy Thursday is more important to me than any chief judgeship. Think no more about it." This is the witness of love, of equity, of justice. No wonder that The Holy Church of Zion was renamed The Church of the Washing of Feet.

PEACE IS A BRIDGE OF LOVE

Peace is a spirit of life, an attitude, before it is an action. As peacemakers, we are first of all persons of inner peace and security in our relationship with God. From this inner harmony between us and God, we are able to extend peace to others. Jesus said, "But I tell you: Love your enemies and pray for those who persecute you, that you may be sons of your Father in heaven" (Matthew 5:44-45).

We do not first avoid violence of deed, but violence of spirit. The key to peacemaking is to be persons of peace, of meekness, of love, who walk above the turbulent waters of distress on a bridge of love.

> Jesus lived a nonresistant lifestyle,
>   turning the other cheek,
>   going the second mile,
>   forgiving the persecutor.
> Jesus is our example of loving others,
>   without coercion,
>   without revenge,
>   in defenselessness.

Turning the other cheek is not a surrender; rather, it is the Christian's strategy of operation, a working philosophy of life.

The only person who is truly free is the one who turns the other cheek. In doing so we are saying, "Your treatment of me does not determine my treatment of you. I am free to act toward you on the basis of principles I have learned from Christ and am enabled to practice by his Spirit and grace."

Our course of action in every situation is not clearly defined—only that it will be an act of love. We have to decide in a given situation what deed will express our freedom to live by love. One thing is clear, we will turn the other cheek, go the second mile, find the way of reconciling love rather than act in retaliation. Love seeks to find the way to rebuild the relationships that have been broken.

There are those who dismiss the Sermon on the Mount as simple idealism, seeing it only as a symbol of the higher life to make us aware that we should never be satisfied with our lesser or sinful roles. This is to rob Jesus of the authenticity of His mission as a teacher, of His role as a discipler. It also serves to excuse us from our responsibility to live in obedience.

For too many people, love is a sentimental feeling and not a course of action. But divine love, God's love which has so reached out to the world as to give his only begotten Son, is an action of sharing, of involvement. Whatever God may "feel," we know His love by His acts of mercy. He is known in history by His acts of deliverance and restoration, and in Jesus Christ in His caring, forgiveness, and reconciliation.

Love reaches across the barrier of our rebelliousness and forgives and restores, builds again the relationship of wholeness. Knowing this love, we too will say, "Like a bridge over troubled waters, I will lay me down. . . . "

PEACE IS REFUSAL TO ACCEPT ALIENATION

Violence begets violence. This is a part of what Jesus meant when He said, "They that take the sword shall perish with the sword." When Martin Luther heard that the reformer Huldrich Zwingli had been killed on the battlefield in a confrontation

143

between his forces and those of Rome, he quoted these words from Jesus, "They that take the sword shall perish with the sword."

When those of us who are Anabaptists visit Zurich, Switzerland, and view the statue of Zwingli by the little church along the Limmat River, we regard the figure of Zwingli holding the sword and the Bible as incongruous. The disciple of Christ is called to live by love, not by violence.

Dr. Harold S. Bender, writing of the Anabaptist vision as the Third Wing of the Reformation defined this vision or movement by three things:

• The rediscovery of the Christian life as discipleship of Christ.

• The recognition that the church is a voluntary community of the reborn.

• The realization that love is the lifestyle for the Christian. It is this third point that expresses the basis for a nonresistant ethic of love.[7] When we know the Prince of Peace as our Lord, we will work together to find answers to hate and violence, injustice and inequity, poverty and illiteracy.

Love doesn't give up, it never fails, it "hangs in" with the person in the problem—all of the way! Jesus "hung in" all of the way to the death. When there are difficulties, we are not to give up on people or write them off. When there are factions in a congregation, far too often there is further division instead of a solution. As a result, all parties suffer; they actually need each other for their greater maturity in the things of Christ. Someone has said that if two persons think exactly alike, one of them is unnecessary!

Peacemaking is a spirit of life that regards persons as more important than preferences. In this spirit we refuse to alienate others by seeking our own way, and we move to reconcile others by seeking a common way. As a friend once said to me, "There are three sides to each issue; his, hers, and the right one!"

To accept alienation as final is to surrender. As in God's dealing with humanity, it isn't God who cuts us off, who washes His hands of the lot of us; it is unrepentant people who cut themselves off by trampling on His love. The gate over the way to hell is a cross, and no one enters there except by tramping over the Son of God. This is the extent to which God expresses His love, and at the most amazing cost to Himself.

PEACE IS THE REJECTION OF VIOLENCE

Jesus came to fulfill, that is, to fill full the law. This is seen in His words:

> You have heard that it was said, "Eye for eye, and tooth for tooth." But I tell you, do not resist an evil person. If someone strikes you on the right cheek, turn to him the other also. And if someone wants to sue you and take your tunic, let him have your cloak as well. If someone forces you to go one mile, go with him two miles. Give to the one who asks you, and do not turn away from the one who wants to borrow from you (Matthew 5:38-42).

His authority is expressed in the words, "It has been said ... but I tell you." He took the Old Testament law, often refered to as *Lex Talionis*, which had been outlined in God's order as a limitation of retaliation to prevent unlimited revenge, and in His sermon presented a higher standard of answering evil with good, of confronting violence with love. This is the Christian's strategy!

The Prophet Isaiah, predicting the coming of the Christ, gave our Lord among other names the title "Prince of Peace." In his prophecy of the "last days," days which the writer of the Hebrews identified with the revelation of God in Jesus (Hebrews 1:2), Isaiah speaks of the peace that will come when people walk in the way of the Lord:

> In the last days the mountain of the Lord's temple will be established as chief among the mountains; it will be raised above the hills, and all nations will stream to it. Many

peoples will come and say, "Come, let us go up to the mountain of the Lord, to the house of the God of Jacob. He will teach us His ways, so that we may walk in His paths." The law will go out from Zion, the word of the Lord from Jerusalem. He will judge between the nations and will settle disputes for many peoples.

They will beat their swords into plowshares and their spears onto pruning hooks. Nation will not take up sword against nation, nor will they train for war anymore. Come, O house of Jacob, let us walk in the light of the Lord (Isaiah 2:2-5, author's italics).

Wherever the Word of God is taken seriously and people follow Christ, they beat their swords into plowshares. As the disciples of Christ, we "walk in the light of the Lord." The truly Christian community espouses an ethic of love, and an ethic of peace, for as disciples of Christ we are committed to live by a Christological ethic. Those of us who name His Name will beat our modern swords and military equipment into plowshares and our spears into pruning hooks! We will begin promoting and producing the things that are for the well-being of the human family.

The church is not producing an ethic for the world but for the Christian commuity. If this separation is lost, and the church seeks to accommodate its ethic to what the world will accept, the church loses the ability to be salt of the earth and the light of the world.

Some who speak of the "fallen world" make the mistake of lowering the Christian ethic by saying that a fallen world can understand us only when we act on the level of fallenness and meet violence with violence. The message of the New Testament is that in Christ this is also a redeemed world, and that as children of God we live by the orders of the redeemed community. The "principalities and powers," according to Paul, will then look in on the redeemed community to discover what God is actually doing in the world (Ephesians 3:10).

The rejection of violence is the first step toward a creative pursuit of reconciliation. As long as violence is our first premise, we cloud the issue, and make it almost impossible to pursue the path of acceptance and arbitration. The way of love means that we rise above violence by reaching out to the other at the risk of being rebuffed, and even at the risk of suffering at his hand.

Calvary stands out in our history as the expression of God's suffering love, of God's own choice of reconciling love as His way of dealing with His enemies.

PEACE IS THE HEALING OF BROKENNESS

One of the beautiful benedictions of the New Testament is found in the Book of Hebrews.

> May the God of peace, who through the blood of the eternal covenant brought back from the dead our Lord Jesus, that great Shepherd of the sheep, equip you with everything good for doing His will, and may He work in us what is pleasing to Him through Jesus Christ, to whom be glory for ever and ever. Amen (13:20-21).

There is an answer to brokenness. There is a balm in Gilead. In God's grace there is acceptance of us as broken and there is forgiveness for us as sinners: "Being reconciled freely by His grace through the redemption that is in Christ Jesus we have peace with God!" As God made peace with us in Jesus, through the cross, so we share peace with others in sharing the cross.

> Peacemaking is done with humility,
> recognizing suffering without being indifferent,
> participating in suffering without anger,
> engaging the suffering without self-defense.
> Peacemaking is done in community,
> in an atmosphere of compassion,
> with a gentleness of common life,
> by a healing of full acceptance.

Healing takes time in the wounded or diseased areas of life. In broken relationships healing takes a healthy input of love, forgiveness, and fellowship for full restoration. In Isaiah 53, we are introduced to the "Wounded Healer" whose identification with us as sinners make possible our healing. The words of the prophet, "by His wounds we are healed," are words of hope, of joy, of assurance. We are made whole through His suffering identification with us.

The Suffering Servant spoken of by the Prophet Isaiah may be described as a Broken Healer. When we meet the Savior at the cross, we discover that He will carry the scars of His love forever. This is the heart of God's "Amazing Grace," that He identifies with humanity even unto death. In those scars, we have assurance that He understands the deepest pains of the human family. Many of us have found that in our suffering we discover a new bond of relationship with others in their suffering, a bond which enables us to also be wounded healers.

PEACE IS THE SHALOM OF GOD

Isaiah said, "The fruit of righteousness will be peace; the effect of righteousness will be quietness and confidence forever. My people will live in peaceful dwelling places, in secure homes, in undisturbed places of rest" (32:17). Righteousness is right-relatedness; it means being brought into right relation with God and, consequently, into right relation with others. This is a relational concept, not a moralistic one. True, there are moral or ethical aspects, for one cannot be in right relation with God without that affecting the "rightness" of the orders of our common life. But the key is the faith-relationship, and we enter this in actuality when we identify with Christ.

To be a disciple is to be in right relatedness with Jesus Christ as our Lord and consequently in actual right relatedness with God. Paul testifies to having once sought his own righteousness, a righteousness of the law, until he met Christ and came into the experience of the righteousness of God; that is, right relatedness with God in Christ (Philippians 3:9).

It is not consistent with the biblical message of reconciliation to reduce salvation to an "insurance policy"—a guarantee that we'll make it to heaven and avoid hell—and miss the fact that salvation is a present relationship with God as our Father. We are now in a new family, we have become a part of the people of God. We are a new community that lives by "righteousness, peace, and joy in the Holy Spirit" (Romans 14:17).

We are a redeemed people, a part of a redeemed community, and as such we live together as a fellowship of the Spirit. The evidence of the Spirit's transforming presence is the fruit that He expresses in our lives. As Jesus taught, He is Himself the vine and we are the branches, and the branch carries nutrition to the fruit, nutrition that comes only from the vine. The only branch that bears fruit is the one attached to the vine.

In the new community of the Spirit, our fruit is the fruit of the Spirit, the life-giving power of His presence and grace. We cannot think fully about such graces as patience, goodness, and peace unless we think of these as the fruit of the Spirit (Galatians 5:22). It is His presence within us that releases the sense of godliness which transforms our lives and makes us become Christlike. This is the wholeness of God!

PEACE IS THE MISSION OF CHRIST

"For to us a Child is born, to us a Son is given, and the government will be upon His shoulders. And He will be called Wonderful Counselor, Mighty God, Everlasting Father, Prince of Peace. Of the increase of His government and peace there will be no end" (Isaiah 9:6-7). The announcement of Jesus' birth included the words, "Peace on earth, to men of good will!" Jesus came as the Prince of Peace, and His ministry brings peace to all of good will.

When Jesus expressed this peace to the disciples, He said that He gives peace not as the world does; He gives an extension of His own peace. The writer of Hebrews calls us to follow peace with all men, and this commandment is placed in the same context as the commandment to follow holiness. In fact, as I stated earlier, the command may be more to follow than to set some particular level of achievement.

In Matthew 10 there is an often quoted word from Jesus, "Think not that I have come to send peace on the earth, I came not to send peace but a sword" (10:34). In the context, Jesus is speaking of the division that His call to discipleship creates in society; some respond and others do not. The sword is this clear separation, and the absence of peace in society does not mean that His promise of peace to His disciples has failed. It means rather that His presence calls for decision, and such a choice creates division. This is expressed four times in the Gospel of John, "There was a division among the people because of Him." As the Prophet Isaiah said, " 'There is no peace,' saith God, 'to the wicked.' " Peace is known fully only as we identify with the Prince of Peace.

Paul expressed his missionary convictions to the Roman Christians, declaring his commitment to come to them on his way to a further mission to Spain. He expresses his sense of mission with a clear conviction of the transforming grace of Christ. He appeals for a spirit of unity among the believers, for acceptance of one another just as Christ became a servant and accepted them, for an authentic experience of joy and peace in the Holy Spirit, and for an obedience to the Spirit that would permit His expressions of divine power in signs and miracles accompanying the proclamation of the Gospel (15:5-24). He concludes the chapter with a reference to the faith of Christ, the love of the Spirit, and the God of peace being their refreshing portion.

Our mission finds its full expression when we bring persons to an understanding of the fullness of God in this way. With Paul, we too have a Gospel of peace, the good news that God is a reconciling God, acting in Christ to reconcile us to Himself. No doubt this is what Ghandi had in mind when he answered the question as to why he didn't confess Christ as Savior, when he regarded his teachings so highly. He replied to E. Stanley Jones in words that are a critique of the Christian community: "When you Christians begin to follow Jesus rather than just worship Him, then something will happen."

One who is at peace within himself can be at peace with others; this is made possible when one is at peace with God. In the peace of God we find assurance, courage, defenselessness, the ability to take risks, the humility to be vulnerable, and the serenity that evidences solidarity with Christ. He is our peace.

8. CONSCIENCE AND SERVICE

Saint Francis of Assisi once said, "Preach the gospel in everything that you do; if necessary, use words." This is the primary goal of serving, to express the good news of grace.

In the spring of 1981 Esther and I moved from Princeton, New Jersey to Washington, D.C., to plant a church. We had spent the winter months at Princeton Seminary, and had been asked by representatives of several mission boards of our church to go to Washington and develop a congregation that would combine the evangelical and the social aspects of the Gospel. In the early years Esther became acquainted with a ghetto family and began a loving service to them, helping them find housing and work, taking the kids to school, securing clothes and other needs, and confronting the husband about his indifference. Later we arranged for the oldest daughter to attend Eastern Mennonite High School. The past six years have seen a lot of service hours invested, but the development in the family, especially in the four children, and their involvement in our church is reward enough. Above all, they are our friends, and they are our associates in the kingdom of Christ.

Freedom to serve is liberation from self-centeredness. The commitment to serve is opposed to the nature of the human ego, for we would rather pursue power. Reinhold Niebuhr analyzes the nature of sin and defines it basically as pride. He states that whether we express our pride in attempts to dominate others by power or by sensuality, the problem is the same, the exploitation of others![1] When one has submitted his/her life to Christ the spirit of life changes, for in this new relation we live to serve Him and all humanity which He serves. The development of a Christian conscience about enabling others will hold us accountable to service in the spirit of Christ.

There is no passage quite so moving in contemplation of this truth as the great Christological passage in the second chapter of Philippians. Here Paul presents the One who was in very nature God, but who became in very nature man and humbled Himself to be a servant, even to the extent of dying on the cross (2:5-11). Paul says that we should let the same mind—the mind of Christ—dominate our lives, guide us in our decisions and relationships, and characterize the spirit in which we serve others.

The church is called to be in society, to be at the cutting edge of life, not by power struggles, but by a quality of life. Someone has said that we have to first be converted from the world to Christ, and then be converted back to the world with Christ. As disciples of Jesus we are engaged in mission, the mission of Christ.

In His service we will avoid perpetuating the status quo and will seek effective ways to apply the meaning of faith to the whole of life. Our service must be creative in interfacing kingdom theology with renewal in the Spirit. We must always be conscious that the power for the new order is the power of the Spirit. Further, our service must be committed to priorities which place the well-being of persons above a legalistic morality, or above purely secular ideals.

It is imperative that we serve for the sake of others and not simply to satisfy something within ourselves that may be calling us to serve. When we serve in the spirit of Christ, we are not fulfilling a legalistic demand but are sharing ourselves with others as a love-action. Unless we face this with honesty, our service itself may be self-serving!

Service is to participate with another,
enabling, equipping,
encouraging, engaging in partnership.
Serving is affirming the other to be
important, worthy,
loved, a partner in pilgrimage.

True service is costly; it involves the giving of ourselves in participation with others. To serve is to say, "Your problem is now my problem, I share it with you." Service means to use our personal power or privilege in the aid of another. Each of us has personal power; the question is whether we use it selfishly to dominate others or unselfishly to enable others. We serve because we have a vision of the ultimate worth of persons.

Can we truly serve another if we have no ultimate concern? Can we love genuinely unless we sense the ultimate worth of personality? Can we effectively serve another unless we consistently think about the need and the wholeness of the other?

Such questions help us to focus on person-centered priorities. But such relationships of meaning are of the spirit of life and not of the intellect alone. We do not hear a symphony with only our minds! Similarly our relationship with God and with other people is not only with our minds.

Whatever we know of genuine service we have learned from our Lord. Jesus said, "The kings of the Gentiles lord it over them; and those who exercise authority over them call themselves benefactors. But you are not to be like that" (Luke 22:25-26). Again, "Whoever wants to become great among you must be your servant" (Matthew 20:27), as the Suffering Servant, who gave Himself to the death for our salvation. As Paul writes regarding the relationship between Christ and the church, "Christ loved the church and gave Himself up for her" (Ephesians 5:25), so it should be in our life in community. We do not simply think about God in our exercise of faith; we surrender ourselves to God, we commit ourselves to serve Him. Christ entered glory through suffering; He achieved power by suffering; He became Master by serving; He overcame sin through the cross; He overcomes evil with good. He creates a kingdom with nonviolence. Christ is King forever, at God's right hand. He is Lord of lords, He is exalted, He is in authority, He is always present. Christ is our Savior, our Lord, and our example!

SERVICE IS ENABLING ONE ANOTHER

El Greco's marvelous painting of the disciple Peter portrays him weeping in anguish. This one scene brings before us the whole story of Peter's love for the Master and his remorse for his unfaithfulness and denial. Similarly, when we meet persons in distress, we find in their attitude a window through which we glimpse the whole person.

Helping a person in difficulty should be done with care and courtesy, with respect and encouragement, and in affirmation of their dignity.

Service to another is an expression of Christian belief that God is not capricious, that He is at work in the world bringing created order out of chaos. As Allan Walker has said of the hope for spiritual renewal, "We confidently look for another of God's creative acts in history." It is with this conviction that we refuse to regard any problem as beyond change, that we function as God's agents of intercession representing Him in the life problems of the needy.

The devaluation of persons is far more serious than the devaluation of money! God calls us to rediscover the essential worth and dignity of persons. This is true not only within the church, but is also applicable to the social and political orders. The remarkable benefits we enjoy should stimulate us to enable others to similar achievements, sharing our resources and expertise. For example, my time in third world countries impresses me that American business could begin with commercial ventures to provide clean water and sewage disposal in every city possible, and thereby enhance the health of the people. But such an endeavor is not at the top of the "INC 500" listing.

God's love enables Him to give Himself for us and to us

without being competitive with us or threatened by us. His purpose is to share for our good, not to use us for a purpose other than the fulfillment of our own personhood. While God calls a people "in and for" community, His love is also shared with each of us personally, because He is personal.

Similarly, we may say that justice is genuine only when it is justice for the individual; and love is genuine only when it is for the individual, for community is made up of individuals who have entered covenant to function in community. We must beware of generalizations about loving and hating that permit us to escape the responsibility to love individuals and to hide from one another in the group. Becoming noncompetitive, we can recognize each others' gifts, affirm one another's value, make others' interests our own. Being noncompetitive, we are free to operate by other principles, to match the adversary with goodness, to serve for the betterment of all.

When we are concerned for Christ's work above all, the important thing is not who does it, but that the work be done. We should be able to support one another in love and prayer as members of the same team. Someone has said, "God is unlimited as to what He can do through the person who doesn't care who gets the credit."

If we believe there is a God, then it is logical for us to let God be God in our lives. It is a farce for us to affirm faith in God and then to engage in practical atheism. The thinking person must work out in his philosophy of life a pattern that recognizes God as the first premise for every consideration. We can paraphrase the first commandment given by God at Sinai as follows: "I am Jehovah your God; all of life is to begin with me."

SERVICE IS MUTUALITY IN LIFE

In Christ, each of us as part of His body is giving visibility to Christ in the world, and each of us is giving visibility for the whole body. We are called to serve each other in humility (1 Peter 5:5), to enable one another rather than to compete.

As a result of theology that does not adequately see Christology as central, we have failed to relate the evangelistic and the social dimensions of the Gospel. We speak of creation, fall, salvation, and consummation as the sweep of God's actions in history and fail to recognize that in Christ, there is a redeemed community in the world expressing the new order.

The new community is one in which we all share together in equality; we recognize and respect one another's gifts; we give and receive from one another both correction and encouragement. We hear one another, that is, complement one another by listening, by hearing not only the words but the heart-cry for understanding, support, and encouragement. Listening takes time; it means being together in empathy and openness and participating with another's dreams and achievements; it involves us in supporting one another where there is a sense of failure or futility.

In Christ we are a new people and members of a new community of disciples. This is not a society of perfectionism. As Bruce Larson is quoted, "You can't be all right and be well. . . . perfectionism will drive you up the wall!" But neither is salvation to be thought of only as an assurance of forgiveness and of a future life; it is to be seen as redemption that reconciles us to God, establishes a new community, and enables a new order of life. As a new people identified with Christ, we will hold each other accountable to live by a Christological ethic.

In a Christological approach to ethics, the righteousness of Christ is effective in the total life. As disciples of Christ, we relate our ethics to Christology in the same way we relate salvation to Christology. That is, we are saved in relation to Christ and we behave our relation to Christ. Love becomes the lifestyle of the disciple. Our service to others is love in action, the service of Christ extended even "to the least of these." Jesus said, "All men know that you are My disciples if you love one another" (John 13:35).

> Compassion is sharing with God,
> it is encounter with God,

it is envisioning God,
it is sharing His kingdom.
Compassion is not elitism,
it is holistic faith,
it is commonness with another,
it is recognizing God's community.

Serving others is to take up the cross in life, to espouse the way of Christ even when it is unpopular. As Christians we have something to say on racism, on materialism, on militarism and the nuclear arms buildup, on abortion and broken marriages, on justice and the plight of the poor. We are called to obedience to Christ.

In service we actualize compassion. We demonstrate that we are here because we care. Service is far beyond the impersonal writing of a check to a charity; it is engaging the persons who could be served by our charity in a manner in which they are recognized as persons of worth far superior to our charity.

Compassion is absolute,
unconditional, total,
persistent, direct.
Compassion is not condescension,
reaching-down sympathy,
indirect pity.
Compassion is perceptive,
receptive, sensitive,
patient, gentle.

SERVICE IS UNSELFISH USE OF PRIVILEGE

Our world needs the good news of a Savior. Elton Trueblood has said that for evidence that we need a Savior, "Go to the gas ovens of the concentration camps; walk down the seared streets of Hiroshima; gaze at the piles of bones and human skulls in Campuchia." Or, I add, watch the drug-pusher destroying teenagers for a few dollars; consider a 747 jumbo-jet crash each week to total the number of those who die from alcohol; observe the brokenness of many homes; or assess the social perversions of violence, militarism, and materialism. We all need a Savior, and having come to know Him we know that Christ needs to be proclaimed!

And we need mentors, persons who model the Christlife in and before society. Holiness is taught by example. Someone has said that the perfume of holiness travels even against the wind. In one of El Greco's paintings, at the bottom right he painted four persons who had influenced him the most — Titian, Michaelangelo, Glovio, and Rubens. Each of us have persons we "paint in" as we think of influences in our lives. As others have served us, so we ought also to be enablers of those with whom we intersect.

Being with people may be the most emotionally costly aspect of service. To serve others, we must meet them where they are. We must to some degree take upon ourselves their life-role for the privilege of authentically entering into it and changing it.

To serve another is to respect their role and their right to our assistance. To serve is to meet them on their turf, to assist them in their pilgrimage and in their becoming. To serve is not to be in charge, but to be charged. One who serves gives up the status of being boss. In serving we share our privilege so that another can participate in the freedoms that we enjoy.

Each of us has personal power if we will but recognize it, strengths that are ours from our heritage, our education, our culture of origin, our family or community, our ability to think, and our training. Wealth and power often include material accumulations, money, property, stocks, job, and so on, but wealth and power are more than that. Unfortunately, some have developed what is being called Dominion Theology, with an emphasis on having dominion in the world, taking power to serve Jesus! What a contrast to the role of the servant.

I have had the privilege of traveling much, with scores of trips to dozens of countries and cultures, and I regard this as wealth. Experience itself is power, especially in some countries of the world where age and gray hair symbolize experience. One can use the wealth of life's enriching experiences for status or for service. Recognition of such privileges as expressions of God's grace to us should lead us to use this wealth in service.

The incarnate Christ became a Servant, even to death on a cross. This is so astounding that it becomes a stumbling block to faith for some, and is of course seen as foolishness by those who are status conscious. The amazement we feel at God's love is expressed in the great hymn by Charles Wesley, "And Can It Be?" and especially in the words of the refrain, "That Thou, my God, shouldst die for me!" This is the ultimate sharing of His personal power for our salvation. Service is placing what you are and have before another for their enrichment.

When we think of the whole Jesus, we recognize that His service of compassionate love was as much a part of His life as His words of exhortation or His death of redemption. We cannot authentically identify with Him unless we identify with the whole Jesus.

SERVICE IS IDENTIFICATION WITH THE NEEDY

As I read the familiar story of the Good Samaritan, I seek to also understand the priest and the Levite. Jesus, the Master Storyteller, wanted His hearers to see the contrast between themselves and the Samaritan. I'm sure they each knew what it was to have a circle of friends and loved ones, but they were selective in their love. In their selectivity the poor man, beaten and robbed, did not figure in their circle of persons who merited love. By the end of the story, Jesus took the lawyer's question, "Who is my neighbor?" and turned it around to ask, "Who is being a neighbor?" This is the question for us. Am I willing to be a neighbor to anyone in need?

The lawyer was seeking a way in which to justify himself, since he professed to love God fully. His love was tied to Torah, to loving the law of God. However, love for God's oracles is not complete without love for God's others, whoever they may be.

The challenge of the story is that love is not fulfilled by affirmations of the mind but by actions of ministry.

The esteemed professor from Hamburg, Germany, Dr. Helmut Thielicke, once wrote to young theologians, "Beware of thinking that when you have read something, you have experienced it." Love is more than an attitude, although it is that; love is an act, a step into relationship.

> Service elevates purpose above position,
> others above self-interest,
> meaning above the material,
> behavior above bargaining.
> Service demonstates our common dignity.

Paul's prayer for the Thessalonians, that their love may abound and overflow, focuses the priority of love in life's relations. Apart from the divine love of *agape* as self-giving, service becomes an obligation engaged in more for what it answers for us than for what it does to help others. We do not serve because of what we get out of it, although service does renew and correct us by the act of self-giving participation; but we serve for the joy of seeing another come into the enjoyment of the kingdom spirit.

Speaking recently at commencement exercises at Taylor University, a historic Christian liberal arts school, I stressed the fact that not only had the student shared in the privilege of being educated in a "Christian community of learning," but that they were going to be enriched by extending this participation in the community of the King all through their lives. To do so they would need to always place purpose above position, character above credentials, and Christ above conventions. This is quality service.

To keep our sense of participation in the community of the King front and center, we will need to keep our relation to Christ clear and authentic. I am not referring to some "sweet Jesus" salvation, primarily internal and self-fulfilling, but to rigorous discipleship with the Jesus who asks us to take up the cross. He is the Master, whom we follow in self-giving service.

SERVICE IS SHAPED BY THE NEED OF OTHERS

The contemporary church continues to separate the evangelical and the social aspects of the Gospel. I believe this results from a basic individualism that keeps us from seeing the broader relationships of the Gospel. If we could think of our mission as people-centered, we would focus that mission holistically. A people-centered approach will bring Christ to people, and will impact the whole person with the whole Christ.

People cannot be dissected into parts, for we are unitary beings. Consequently, we cannot minister to the mind apart from the personality, nor to the soul apart from the body. The good news is that we want people to enjoy what Christ has for them in this life, as well as in the future!

Christian faith does not follow the Greek dualism that separated the physical and the spiritual. As in the Hebrew tradition, Christian faith regards persons as unitary beings, each as one integrated personality. The physical, emotional, intellectual, spiritual, and relational aspects of life are all a part of one unitary being. Physical well-being is not unimportant; yet when health is lacking we are not left without other resources.

Service is often a ministry to material needs as well as to spiritual needs, and as such is a valid expression of the Christian faith. We should not so readily separate the spiritual from the material, the inner piety from the outward performance, the redemptive from the ethical. The New Testament calls us to a holistic approach to faith, bringing our very bodies to God as living sacrifices, our "spiritual worship" (Romans 12:1).

Paul commended his friends for supplying his physical needs and acknowledged their gifts as a valid ministry extended by the church. He saw their material giving as an act of service which also refreshed his spirit.

As Jesus moved among the people, He saw them as "sheep having no shepherd," as the field "white and ready for harvest," as the blind being led by the blind, as the poor and dispossessed, as the hungry crowd who had no bread, as persons without hope. He came announcing the kingdom of God, but also personifying the kingdom in His person and life. He came to seek and to save that which was lost, to give His life a ransom for many, to reconcile humanity to the Father. His giving, His serving, was with the full recognition of the cost of suffering; the cross was not unexpected, but was the way of suffering love.

Jesus was moved with compassion,
    feeling their hunger more deeply,
    sensing their lostness more fully,
    knowing their problem more truly.
The greatness of His love is in sharing Himself.

Jesus' compassion is not weakness;
    it chooses to be powerless with the powerless,
    it chooses to walk with the less fortunate,
    it reaches out to help the dispossessed.
Jesus' compassion is kind to those who are hurting.

In suffering, just to know that someone notices and cares is in itself an encouragement. We can do more when we do not feel alone. In the midst of despair, it helps to have someone reach out a caring hand. In despondence of spirit and gripped by futility, we feel new strength when we hear a word of hope. We serve others best by a love that identifies and provides enabling, not by a superior act that intimidates or makes one dependent.

Service is the evidence that we understand another's place in life. Service moves to another. Service identifies with another. Service says,

"I see you,
    "I feel with you,
        "I care about you,
            "I will identify with you,
                "I will share myself with you."

We do not move into another's life and take over their role in their problems, for this would be to depersonalize them. Rather, we move in to participate and to help them cope with and actually transform their relationship to problems.

We grow as individuals as we work through difficulties, and we can grow with another in their growing, a growth that happens as we share with them. Of our Lord, the Scripture says, "He learned obedience from what He suffered and, once made perfect, He became the source of eternal salvation" (Hebrews 5:8-9).

Compassion is learned, because it is the opposite of our basic self-centeredness. I remember a college librarian, Miss Sadie Hartzler, saying, "We learn compassion by being with people in need, or by being close to someone who has friends who are in need." We can be taught by the Spirit through our moving among people in need, or we can be taught by being prayerfully close to God and participating in His compassion for humanity. But we must recognize that compassion is a calling that is not native to our self-interests. How marvelous that God is shown throughout the Testaments as a God of steadfast love, of compassion and caring. The psalmist says, "Like as a father pitieth his children, even so the Lord pitieth them that fear Him" (Psalm 103:12).

SERVICE IS THE PRACTICE OF LOVE

Mozart was asked what he was trying to express by his music. He replied, "If I could express it in words, I would not need music!"

As a sculptor, my wife, Esther, has often made the same statement about her art. In a similar way, love is its own language. We express love-words, yes, but love acts. There is a language of touch, of tenderness, of worth that is other than words. Service is a language, a symbol of communication of worth, of dignity, of love to another person. In serving another we are saying, "I love you deeply enough to cut you into my life!" We may not speak eloquently, but there is an eloquence of fellowship that will outlive the words the service embodies.

The Suffering Servant emptied Himself;
this is the price of serving,
the cost of humility before others,
the liberation from idolizing status.
The disciple empties himself to become a servant.

To "empty oneself" is strange language for most of us. Our lives are so full that we have no room for others. In the Western world, we order our lives by the clock and the calendar; we sell time by the hour or half-hour; and even conversation with another is controlled by the clock. And we are scheduled—how we are scheduled—by the day, the week, the month, and some of us by the year for years ahead! If we would serve others, we must begin by emptying ourselves of the interests which hold priority, we must make room for the other and give ourselves fully, genuinely, unselfishly, completely to another.

Love is like a skill course, for one grows in love by practicing love. Further, love enlarges the soul of the lover, for in the act of loving we become more capable of love. The selfish person is incapable of receiving and giving love. It is in giving that we receive, in sharing that we participate with the other, and in opening ourselves to others we are in turn enriched by them.

Love is to be genuine, without hypocrisy. It is to be transparent, without selfish interest. Love is self-giving for the good shared with others. Love enriches another, bringing a sense of worth and meaning; love brings a fullness, even when life is empty of many things. And what are things, if we have persons we love and who love us? Here is our greater wealth—the wealth of friends, of persons who share love.

Edgar Guest attended a dinner party. Before the dinner, he was seated in the drawing room beside a millionaire. As people came and went, one after another spoke to Edgar Guest, exchanging pleasantries. The millionaire suddenly said, "It seems that you have many friends and I have none." Guest responded,

165

"While you were busy making money, I was making friends!"

SERVICE IS AN EXPRESSION OF WORTH

Paul wrote to the Galatians, "You, my brothers, were called to be free. But do not use your freedom to indulge the sinful nature; rather, serve one another in love. The entire law is summed up in a single command: "Love your neighbor as yourself" (5:13-14).

G.K. Chesterton, writing of St. Francis of Assisi, said, "He treated the whole mob of men as a mob of kings!"[2] Not any one of us is an ordinary citizen in the kingdom of God. Each one is important to God; consequently, each person should be important to us. No one should be outside of our circle of concern. We are sent into the world by Christ just as the Father sent Him into the world as an expression of divine love (John 20:21).

In Christ we are made new creatures, reconciled to God by His grace. Now we are ambassadors for Christ, for He has committed to us the word and the work, the message and the ministry of reconciliation (2 Corinthians 5:17-20). As agents of His reconciling love, we are heralds of the kingdom, participants of the new community of the King.

Commitment to Christ and His life
is not withdrawl but a different engagement,
is not identity with the world but selectivity,
is not antagonism but compassion,
is not isolation but separation,
Commitment to Christ is beyond surrender to sanctity.

Commitment to Christ is discipleship
in faithfulness to His Word,
in walking in His Spirit,
in loving in His style,
in relating by His justice,
Commitment to Christ is living in His peace.

With a world of over five billion people, an urbanization of many societies that results in cities with wall-to-wall people, with individualism and anonymity as characteristics of urbanism, there is increased relevance to service as an affirmation of worth. No person is unimportant. No person is to be taken for granted. Not only must we avoid sins of commission but sins of omission. None of us likes to be ignored, we all want to be noticed, affirmed, and counted to be important.

The opposite of love is not wrath but indifference. God's wrath is the other face of His love; it is the act of love refusing to coerce or manipulate another person while at the same time expressing one's rejection of the person's action. Wrath is love's exposure of another's mistake; it is the expression of caring deeply about another. Indifference is the opposite of love, saying that the other is not important. To love is to care, to share, even to expose the error that will hurt. But love's wrath is not vengeance, for love's exposure precludes taking vengeance. Love's wrath is taking the other seriously for himself and holding him accountable. Actually, God's wrath is more a withdrawing of Himself in response to the person's rejection of Him than it is an overt act of revenge. Divine vengeance is a retribution that only God can render justly, for it is His respect for the human decision to reject God. When a human insists upon independence from God, persists in his rejection of God, the nature of love means that God will not impose Himself upon the person but respects the persons freedom to say no to Him. This total abandonment is God's wrath.

God's wrath is the other side of His love, it is His refusal to violate human freedom, leaving the person the choice of isolation from God. Yet God continues to be merciful, extending His mercy on the just and the unjust. His expression of mercy is a call for thinking persons to reconsider their stance.

SERVICE IS A BRIDGE ACROSS CULTURES

Peter's call to minister to Cornelius in Acts 10 is a wonderful bridge of love.

As Peter entered the house, Cornelius met him and fell at his feet in reverence. But Peter made him get up. "Stand up," he said, "I am only a man myself." Talking with him, Peter went inside and found a large gathering of people. He said to them: "You are well aware that it is against our law for a Jew to associate with a Gentile or visit him. But God has shown me that I should not call any man impure or unclean. So when I was sent for, I came without raising any objection" (10:25-29).

In missiology we focus on contextualization. We have moved beyond the concern for indigenization to seek authentic ways of contextualizing. Our challenge is to express the meaning of the Gospel of God's kingdom in other cultures. While this involves the choice of verbal symbols that will be understood in another culture, more deeply than the use of words it involves contextualizing meaning in the receiving culture.

One language that bridges between cultures is the spirit and deed of love. Even the smile, a gracious and courteous manner of relating to people, speaks beyond the language facility. In our travels and ministry in many countries of the world, I've needed to work through an interpreter—or interrupter! In most settings, I have had interpreters who have not only translated my words but who have caught my meanings and expressed them in their own language's word-pictures.

During our three months of teaching at Union Biblical Seminary in Pune, India in 1987, my wife communicated by her gift as a sculptor. She designed and constructed a nine-foot tall concrete sculpture of Jesus washing a disciple's feet. It is made of poured concrete covered with a final coat of white cement with Italian marble chips, in appearance as a marble sculpture. This semiabstract work is a statement that is understood in that context. It speaks without words to all who come to the campus.

We shall long remember the amazement of the Muslim army official who stood before the sculpture, asking numerous questions of its meaning. Suddenly he said, "But you Christians claim that Jesus is God. God would never have stooped down and washed a person's feet!" To this, Esther replied that we believe that God came to us in Jesus, in self-giving love, forgiving us and accepting us as His own, and that He did express this love by washing the disciples' feet. He stood in silent thought for a few moments, then he shook his head in amazement at the thought of Jesus stooping to serve another in such a menial way, and walked away pondering.

In our world we think of power as an expansion of life; but in the Christian message we learn that power limits life to what one controls, while loving service goes on expanding. It enriches the one serving as well as the ones being served.

> Service expands one's life
> by including others,
> by extending one's resources,
> by sharing personal power.
> Service enhances the good
> by joining hands as partners,
> by adjusting to common need,
> by enriching the common life.

Service to one another is an expression of community, of our being participants together in the pilgrimage of life. Contrary to our western individualism, there is greater strength to be found in life together. Rather than insulate ourselves against one another, or separate ourselves from one another we should discover the exhilaration of togetherness, the dynamic of community.

In the global community, the church needs to lead the way in overcoming the individualism that keeps us from helping one another. The mood of human nature is more one of competition than one of community. While we need one another, and we are dependent upon one another for the larger and more fulfilling aspects of life, we back away from serving one another in a quest to preserve our own self-interests. When we discover in God's grace the meaning of self-giving love, of serving others, we will be rewarded by the joy of mutual service.

SERVICE IS WASHING ANOTHER'S FEET

Following the days of the Cultural Revolution in China, and the long imprisonment of many Christians, a group of pastors who had just been released from prison were asked what sustained them in their difficult times. They referred to the story from the Gospel of John relating the act of Jesus washing the feet of his disciples, apparently including Judas, as giving them support in accepting their persecutors and being gracious to them.

Some of us would serve if we could do it in our own living rooms, in our own way. When serving means that we meet the needs of others where they are found, we find it distasteful.

Many would like to make the spiritual life into some mystical sacrament by which we escape from real life, but Jesus calls us to feed the hungry, bring drink to the thirsty, give hospitality to the homeless, clothe the poor, and visit the sick and the imprisoned (Matthew 25:34-45). Such deeds are not easily glorified; they are commonplace. But when done in the spirit of Christ they are uncommon deeds done to very common persons!

> Obedience is the heartbeat of service,
>   Love-response that is unconditional,
>   Love-sharing that is unlimited,
>   Love-service that is unrestrained.
> Obedience is faithfulness to our Savior.

To wash another's feet is to bring refreshing to the weary, to bring cleansing to the defiled, and to give acceptance to others. In taking the servant role voluntarily, when it is not our social lot, we dignify this role to our peers by our example. We bring the servant role into the consciousness of peers who may have taken need for granted and been unconscious of those living in social powerlessness.

We need to be more conscious of the different gifts people bring by their service. We are interdependent, enriched by one another. We not only think of serving, but we should honestly recognize how much we are served by others. None of us is

170

complete in and of ourselves, we are completed by others.

Each society has its coolies, its working class who perform functions without which our privileges in life would be radically altered. When we love people, we care for them; we not only notice them, but we respect and appreciate them. It is in people, not in impersonal nature, that we find our greater appreciation of God's handiwork. While I'm a lover of nature, enjoying the hills and valleys, the forests and the mountains, the streams and lakes, especially with my hobby of Canada geese and white mute swan, yet it is in the faces of people, black and white, on the streets of Washington that I see the image of God.

It is said of Bombay, India that if the slums were removed the city would collapse economically. We are dependent upon one another and indebted to one another. Jesus calls us to walk among the peoples of the different social levels with a sense of community, with acknowledgement of the human worth and dignity seen in each individual, and with the love that will serve any one of them in the spirit of Christ.

SERVICE IS KINGDOM MISSION

The message of the Bible is the story of God acting to reconcile a people to Himself, of God calling us in grace to be a redeemed community inviting others to share this experience of grace. As Theodore Wedel speaks of this mission he emphasizes the three words of a French evangelistic group: presence, service, and communication. We are a presence for Christ, we serve in the spirit of Christ, and thereby we earn the right to be heard.

It is said that a reporter followed Mother Teresa through a day of her roles in service. At the end of the day he said, "I wouldn't do what you do for a million dollars." She replied, "Neither would I!"

As I think of evangelism, from thirty-five years of many evangelistic missions, I have arrived at a definition for evangelism that is satisfying to me. Evangelism is everything that makes faith in Christ a possibility for a person. This definition does not separate deed from word, act from articulation, the evangelical from the social aspects of mission. Evangelism should be the highest service to others, not a professional role nor a position of status in the church.

> Service calls for clarity on vocation:
>   for our vocation is not occupation.
>   We have one vocation in Christ,
>   we are called to discipleship,
>   we are a community of disciples.
> Service extends vocation into career;
>   vocation selects and enriches occupation,
>   sanctifying it as a service for God,
>   safeguarding it from competition,
>   securing it as an extension of Christ's goal.

We need to rediscover the primacy of vocation as the Christian's calling, as our role of discipleship. Our occupation finds its direction from our vocation, for our vocation becomes the guide for selectivity in occupation and in the quality of performance. By serving effectively we condition persons to hear the interpretation of our lives, our faith, and the meanings by which we live. Service is an integral part of our mission.

> The church is the "body of Christ,"
>   the visible expression of Christ in society,
>   the demonstration of community,
>   the fellowship of freedom, holiness, and joy,
>   the congregation of the repentant spirit.
> The church witnesses by practicing love.

> The church is people, not building;
>   sharing in congregational discernment,
>   making Spirit-directed decisions,
>   reviewing and engaging in missions,
>   nurturing and disciplining one another.
> The church worships in the presence of Christ.

When we as God's people gather to worship it is not as a gathering of people who have been sinning all week and need a release and therapy for freedom, but we gather as people who have walked with Christ all week and have come together to celebrate and to find revitalization for His service in the coming week. This is not to say that we have not sinned in the past week, although having committed our lives to Christ the rebellion of sin was brought to an end and we do not repeat that rebellion, but as we day by day face our sins honestly we come together in worship as forgiven sinners who have met for the joy of fellowship and praise, for the exercises of nurture and the refocusing of our mission.

Theologian David Bosch, who has lived in the pain of the South Africa experience, addressed a conference of the National Initiative for Reconciliation in Pietermaritzburg, South Africa in September 1985, on "An Afrikaner's thoughts on reconciliation."[3] His address contained twelve theses which express the heart-cry of an Afrikaner Christian who longs for reconciliation in a crisis-torn land.

1. Cheap reconciliation is the deadly enemy of the church.

2. All of us are prisoners of history, and are challenged to become prisoners of hope.

3. The biblical concept of reconciliation has as its corollaries the concepts of repentance and forgiveness.

4. In ordinary human communication, people are usually more aware of the sins of others than of their own sins.

5. In the context of the Christian faith, by contrast, we judge ourselves before we judge others.

6. If we are followers of the one who was crucified, we too will have to be cross-bearers.

7. Repentance and conversion always affect those elements in our lives that touch us most deeply, which you are most attached and devoted to, without which, so we believe, we simply cannot live.

8. Confession of guilt and repentance cannot be imposed by others but is a gift of the Holy Spirit.

9. Our most terrible guilt is that of which we are unaware.

173

10. God forgives us our debts as we also forgive our debtors.

11. If we reject the road of reconciliation, we are crucifying Christ anew.

12. Reconciliation is not a human possibility, but ultimately, finally, a divine gift.

We are ambassadors for Christ with a ministry and message of reconciliation. He has committed to us the word and the work of being His agents of reconciliation in society. As ambassadors we take our directions from our Sovereign, and we go to the persons of influence and leadership among the people to whom we are sent, and from that base we begin a service to the whole society, demonstrating by our service that we serve all persons equally.

As we represent Christ in life we do so best by walking with Him in transparency. This is an honesty which is shown both in how we deal with our failures and how we find strength for our successes. Whatever is achieved of lasting significance is a gift of God's grace. Yet we are to personify this grace, for He works in and through us. Service, like holiness, is not taught by words but by example. But our service is not just altruism; it is in the name and Spirit of Christ. The evidence that He is our Master is in the fact that we are His servants. Our identity is in Christ!

finis

ENDNOTES

Chapter 1

1 John Howard Yoder, *The Politics of Jesus* (Grand Rapids: Eerdmans, 1972).

2 Søren Kierkegaard, *Purity of Heart Is to Will One Thing* (New York: Harper and Row, 1956).

Chapter 2

1 Paul Tournier, *Guilt and Grace* (New York: Harper and Row, 1962).

2 John Driver, *Understanding the Atonement for the Mission of the Church* (Scottdale, Pennsylvania: Herald Press, 1986), 179.

3 *Ibid.*

4 Gustav Aulen, *Christus Victor* (New York: Macmillan, 1969).

Chapter 3

1 Faith Martin, *Call Me Blessed* (Grand Rapids: Eerdmans, 1989).

2 "Die Bergpredigt, no. 105 of *Theologische Existenz Heute* (Munich: Kaiser Verlag, 1963).

Chapter 4

1 St. Augustine, *Confessions I*, 6; newly translated by Albert Outler (Philadelphia: Westminster, 1955).

2 John Baillie, *Christian Devotion* (New York: Scribners), 15–16.

3 David Bosch, *A Spirituality of the Road* (Scottdale, Pennsylvania: Herald Press, 1979), 17.

4 Abraham Kuyper, *Lectures on Calvinism* (Grand Rapids: Eerdmans, 1943), 29.

5 Kosuke, *No Handles on the Cross* (London: SCM Press, 1976), 75.

6 E. Stanley Jones, *The Unshakable Kingdom* (Nashville: Abingdon Press, 1972), 16.

7 *Ibid.*, 42.

Chapter 5
1 John Driver, *Understanding the Atonement for the Mission of the Church* (Scottdale, Pennsylvania: Herald Press, 1986), 36.
2 James D. Hunter, *Evangelicals, the Coming Generation* (University of Chicago Press, 1987).
3 Lesslie Newbigin, *Foolishness to the Greeks* (Grand Rapids: Eerdmans, 1986).

Chapter 6
1 Elton Trueblood, *A Place to Stand* (New York: Harper and Row, 1969), 28.
2 *Leadership '88 Letter,"* Vol. 1, No. 4, (Pasadena, California: Lausanne Committee).
3 Catholic Bishops, *Pastoral Letter,* 1986.
4 "Lausanne Covenant," (Minneapolis: World Wide Publications, 1975), paragraph 9.
5 CMS News Letter, No. 374, May 1974.
6 John Dresscher, *The Way of the Cross and Resurrection* (Scottdale, Pennsylvania: Herald Press, 1978), 72.
7 Emil Brunner, *Justice and the Social Order* (New York: Harper and Row, 1945), 196.
8 John Dresscher, *The Way of the Cross and Resurrection* (Scottdale, Pennsylvania: Herald Press, 1978), 214,

Chapter 7
1 Lukas Haas, unpublished letters.
2 Martin Luther King, *Strength to Love* (New York: Harper and Row, 1963), 40.
3 Jacques Ellul, *Violence* (New York: Seabury, 1962).
4 See Hendrick Berkhof, *Christ and the Powers* (Scottdale, Pennsylvania: Herald Press, 1962).
5 *The New Book of Christian Quotations* (New York: Crossroad, 1982).
6 For the text of the Schleitheim Confession, see John Howard Yoder, *The Legacy of Michael Sattler* (Scottdale, Pennsylvania: Herald Press, 1973).

Chapter 8

1 Reinhold Niebuhr, *The Nature and Destiny of Man* (New York: Scribners, 1946), 94.

2 David Bosch, *Heal the Land* (Monrovia, California: MARC Publishers, September 1985).